Female Foeticide

A Legal Approach

Female Foeticide

A Legal Approach

Lt. (Dr.) Reeta Nigam

Delta Book World
New Delhi-110 002

First Published in 2018
ISBN 978-93-85719-05-9

Published by **Abhishek Goel** on behalf of

Delta Book World
G-4, Prahlad House
4832/24, Ansari Road
New Delhi - 110 002 (India)

Tel.: 011-4707 2321, 2324 5799
E-mail: deltabookworld@gmail.com
Website: www.kaveribooks.com

PRINTED IN INDIA

Preface

"*Yatra Naryaste Pujuanthe Raman the Tatra Devatha*" has been the culture of India. In India, a girl is worshiped as a *Devi* on one hand and denied her existence on the other as if she has no right to live.

Female foeticide in India is genocide of one million women annually with tragic consequences. It is the abortion of a female foetus outside the legal methods. The child sex ratio is within the normal ratio range in all eastern and southern states of India but significantly higher in certain western and particularly northern western states such as Maharashtra, Haryana and Jammu & Kashmir (118, 120 and 116 as of census of 2011 respectively). The western states of Maharashtra and Rajasthan, 2011 census found a child sex ratio of 113, Gujarat 112 and Uttar Pradesh 111.

The Indian census data suggests there is a positive correlation between abnormal sex ratio and better socio-economic status and literacy. This may connected to the dowry system in India where dowry deaths occur when a girl is seen as financial burden. Urban India has higher child sex ratio than rural India according to 1991, 2001 and 2011 census data.

The Mumbai High Court ruled that pre-natal sex determination implied female foeticide, sex determination violated a woman's right to live and was against Indian constitution (UNICEF India).

The *Beti Bachao* or 'Save Girl Child' campaign has been underway in many Indian communities since the early 2000s.

There is an ongoing debate as to whether this high sex ratio are only caused by female foeticide or some of the other higher ratio is explained by natural causes. The Indian government has passed Pre-Conception and Pre-Natal Diagnostic Techniques Act (PCPNDT) in 1994 to ban and punish pre-natal sex screening and female foeticide. It is currently illegal in India to determine or disclose sex of the foetus to anyone. However there are concerns that PCPNDT Act has been poorly enforced by authorities.

It is needed to take urgent steps to end immediately this genocide and prevent its tragic consequences. Only legislation enacted on this behalf is not sufficient. Orthodox views regarding women need to be changed.

Lt. (Dr.) Reeta Nigam

Contents

1

Introduction

"Female infanticide is the intentional killing of baby girls due to preference for male babies and from the low value associated with the birth of females". It should be seen as a subset of the broader phenomenon of infanticide, which has also targeted the physically or mentally handicapped, and infant males (alongside infant females or, occasionally, on a gender-selective basis). As with maternal mortality, some would dispute the assigning of infanticide or female infanticide to the category of "genocide" or, as here, "gendercide." Nonetheless, the argument advanced in the maternal mortality in a case- study holds true as well : governments and other actors can be just as guilty of mass killing by neglect or tacit encouragement, as by direct murder. R.J. Rummel Buttresses[1] this view, referring to infanticide as another type of government killing whose victims may total millions.... In many cultures, government permitted, if not encouraged, the killing of handicapped or female infants or otherwise unwanted children. In the Greece of 200 B.C., for example, the murder of female infants was so common that among 6,000 families living in Delphi no more than one percent had two daughters. Among 79 families, nearly as many had one child as two. Among all there were only 28 daughters to 118 sons.... But classical Greece was not unusual. In eighty-four societies spanning the Renaissance to our time, "defective" children have been killed in one-third of them. In India, for example, because of Hindu beliefs and the rigid caste system, young girls were murdered as a matter of course. When demographic statistics were first collected in the nineteenth century, it was discovered that in "some villages, no girl babies were found at all; in a total of thirty others, there were 343 boys to 54 girls... Bombay, there were 603 girls were alive in 1834.

It is a disgrace for the Indian society, which considers the birth of a girl child as a bad investment in future. The Atharvaveda says, "The birth of a daughter, grant it elsewhere, here grant a son". This saying in the holy scripture sums up the Indian attitude towards children who are subjected to multifarious travails inflicted by the society on them. The girl children in India have been the most vulnerable for centuries and are even today, vulnerable to the insults of deprivation as well as discrimination. Whatever the natural biological laws of human reproduction had given mankind for balancing its natural sex ratio, has been taken away by man made laws, customs, traditions, religious beliefs and sophisticated medical technology, resulting in a lower status in society for girls as well as women. For too long have they been left on the back burner, facing discrimination throughout their entire journey from cradle to the grave. In particular, peculiar to South Asia, and certainly to India, tradition values and customs encrusted over time have resulted in the insatiable desire for sons, with families having totally marginalized the joy and pleasure in giving birth to a baby girl.

It is agonizing to know that the gender bias and deep-rooted prejuidice and discrimination against girl child, which have been there down the centuries, are now found to begin in the womb itself. The girl child in the womb faces the peril of prebirth elimination i.e. female foeticide. She is considered to be consumer rather than a producer, and this narrow viewpoint of the Indian patriarchal society has lead to horrid practices like female infanticide and female foeticide. Escalating demands of dowry was cited as the main reason for it. Daughters were unable to provide social security to parents and called for unnecessary investment on themselves, the fruits of which were taken away by the in-laws.

The decline in sex ratio might lead to degradation of moral values in the society resulting in polyandry, violence against women, red trafficking etc.

The latest advances in modern medical sciences – the tests like amniocentesis and ultrasonography are being abused. The tests which were originally designed for the detection of gender related congenital abnormality of the foetus are now being abused particularly in India and Asian countries primarily to detect the sex of the foetus with the intention of getting it aborted if it happens to be that of a female. Such foetus is considered to be "suffering from the very disease of being a female foetus". If the female foetus is lucky enough to survive till her birth then she faced the peril of elimination in infancy by female infanticide. Kolloor defined it as, "Killing of an entirely dependent girl child under one year of age by mother, parents or others in whose care she is entrusted". Historically, female infanticide has been in existence since long. Girl infant have been known to be killed by rubbing poison on the mother's breast, by feeding infants with milk of errukam flower or oleander berries, by using sap of calotropis plant, paddy grains, giving sleeping tablets or by simply burying the girl infants alive. Law banned this heinous practice in 1870, more than a century ago. Yet this abuse of girl child which is violation of her human right to life, continues to prevail not only in some parts of Rajasthan and Gujarat but recently has been found in some districts of Tamil Nadu and Maharashtra as well.

Sex determination tests are seen as providing a 'reproductive choice'– a choice to decide to have a boy or a girl. However women do not really enjoy an unfettered choice. Choice cannot exist in the context where women are socialized to subordinate their interests to those of men; where women attain a status only through marriage and by giving birth to children preferably sons; where they largely bear the burden of cooking, collecting firewood, fetching water, bearing and rearing children, tending cattle; eat last and the least, have lesser access to education and health services. Choice is only meaningful if it can be exercised in the context of material, social and gender equity. The availability of sex detection tests creates a situation where women are forced to undergo the test either by external pressure from family members or by internalized social values.

The supporters of sex detection tests argue that on the basis of the theory of demand and supply, an excess of males over females achieved with the reduction of unwanted, and hence, neglected female children would actually raise the status of women. However if mere numbers were to indicate status, then in several states in India, where adverse sex ratio exists, status of women would be high. On the contrary, one observes that incidence of dowry deaths, rape and other atrocities being committed in these states is as high as in other states. Based on anthropological evidence it has been observed that societies with adverse female sex ratio have indicated the presence of customs like polyandry and abduction and purchase of women. It is strongly felt, that contrary to raising the status of women, adverse sex ratio would increase the incidence of rape, prostitution and violence against women.

Meaning

Female Foeticide is still a problem in 21st century India. It still continues to be unabated in parts of India. Modern technology combined with a cultural preference for sons rather than daughters has led to the mushrooming of neo-natal clinics across India where parents can check the sex of their unborn child. In some parts of the country parents are choosing to abort if the child is female.

The ineffective implementation of the legislation is evident in India's skewed gender ratio. According to the decennial census, carried out in 2001, the ratio for 0-6 year-olds fell from 945 females per 1,000 males in 1991 to 927 in 2001 and 919 in 2011 one of the lowest in the world.

Contrary to popular perception that the deeply rooted prejudice against girls, reflected in the country's sex ratio, is mostly in rural areas, some of the largest cities in India - including Delhi and Mumbai - has inbalanced sex ratio in 2011 Census.

In 2011, for every 1000 boys aged 0-6 years, there were 852 girls in Mumbai, 832 girls in Delhi and 942 girls in Hyderabad (according 2011 census).

What is Female Foeticide?

Female foeticide refers to the abortion of a fetus of female gender as a result of a sex-determination test. Both female foeticide (also referred to as sex-selective abortion) and sex-determination tests are illegal in India. However, abortion is legal. Abortion is allowed if the pregnancy does not exceed 12 weeks (3 months)[2], and it is also allowed if pregnancy does exceed 12 weeks but does not exceed 20 weeks under the conditions that:

(i) the continuance of the pregnancy would involve a risk to the life of the pregnant woman or of grave injury to her physical or mental health; or

(ii) there is a substantial risk that if the child were born, it would suffer from such physical or mental abnormalities to be seriously handicapped.

(Out of the many arguable causes of Female Foeticide, the abortion laws also take their share of blame.)

Sex of a fetus can only be determined with an ultrasound scan at 18-20 weeks of pregnancy:

> A baby's sex can be seen on ultrasound starting at about 18 to 20 weeks, but not all babies co-operate with the scan your baby has to be in a position to allow the scan operator to see the male or female parts. And mistakes can be made even if people do get a good view of the baby's sex – there are no guarantees.

Therefore, sex-selective abortions must occur close to 20 weeks or after 20 weeks. Despite being illegal, sex-selective abortions also fall in the grey area of the abortion law as well. Most of these abortions are not reported for obvious legal complications; thus, lack of recorded evidence that they happen except the abysmal sex ratio for 0-6 age group and occasional discoveries of female fetuses thrown away to rot.

Female foeticide is spreading like an epidemic in our society.

There is fast decrease in the population of women in our country. In 1961 census the sex ratio was 941 but in the census 2001 it is decreased to 933 per thousand.[3] While the child sex ratio between age group of 0-6 it is 927 in 2001 and 919 in 2011 per thousand.[4] According to a study conducted by United Nation Children's Fund (UNICEF) near about 50 million girls are excluding from the India population. There is continuous decline in the sex ratio from the year 1961 but maximum in the decade 1991-2001. There is drastic decline in child sex ratio in Punjab state where it is 800 girls to 1000 boys. The social, cultural and religious fiber of India is pre-dominantly patriarchal contributing extensively to the secondary status of women. The patrilineal social structure based on the foundation that the family runs through a male and makes male a precious commodity that needs to be protected and given special status. Another important pillar of the patriarchal structure is marriage wherein women are given sub-ordinate status having no say in the running of their life or any control over their body or bodily integrity. Marriage is also considered as a process where by the burden of the father is passed on to the husband for a very high price. The dowry or groom price is so staggeringly high irrespective of the class structure that generations may have to toil to repay the debts incurred during marriage. All of this has contributed to a low status for women in the society to such an extent that even the birth of a girl child in a family is sought to be avoided. A deleterious fall out of the subjugated position of women is their vulnerability to violence, rape, sexual abuse, dowry harassment, domestic violence, trafficking etc with little or no mechanisms of combating the same either by way of effective laws and implementation or civil society action. Various methods were found to eliminate the girl child after her birth like starving her, crushing her under bed or giving poison etc. Pertinently the responsibility for killing the child was fixed on the mother/women as she was considered responsible for bringing the girl child into existence. The causes for elimination of girl child indicate that the reasons are similar and different depending upon the geographical location in which female infanticide is practiced. An exorbitant dowry demand is one of the main reasons for female infanticide. Some of the other reasons are the belief that it is only the son who can perform the last rites, lineage and inheritance runs through the male line, sons will look after parents in old age, men are bread winners etc. Strong male preference and the consequent elimination of the female has continued to increase rather than decline with the spread of education.

Status of Women

The adverse sex ratio has been linked with the low status of women in Indian communities, both Hindu and Muslim. The status of women in a society can be determined by their education, economic role, presence in the profession and decision-making power within the family. It is deeply influenced by the beliefs and values of society. Among Hindus, preference for the male child is likewise deeply enshrined in belief and practice. The Ramayana and the Manusmriti (the Laws of Manu) represent the ideal woman as obedient and submissive, and always needing the care of a male: first father, then husband, then son. Religion operates alongside other cultural and economic factors in lowering the status of women. The practice of dowry has spread nationwide, to communities and castes in which it had never been the custom. In the majority of cases, the legal system has no impact on the practice of dowry. It is estimated that a dowry death occurs in India every hour.[5]

The need for a dowry for girl children, and the ability to demand a dowry for boys exerts considerable economic pressure on families to use any means to avoid having girls.

Women and Developments in Reproductive Technology, Abortion was legalized in India in 1971 (Medical Termination of Pregnancy Act) to strengthen humanitarian values.

Situation in India: Facts and Figure

The latest Census shows that the juvenile sex ratio, which had become a concern in the 1991 Census, has gone down even further. In 1991, the national average for the child sex ratio, in the

0-6 age-group, was 945. Several states, including Punjab, Haryana, Himachal Pradesh and Uttar Pradesh had fewer than 900 girls per 1,000 boys. However in Census 2001 in Punjab, Haryana, Himachal Pradesh and Gujarat alone, the sex ratio had plunged. In 1991, all districts of Punjab except Nawanshahr, recorded a child sex ratio lower than 900. In the 2001 Census, while Nawansahar recorded a child sex ratio of 810 girls per 1,000 boys, more alarmingly, 10 of the 17 districts of Punjab recorded fewer than 800 girls per 1,000 boys.

The past decade also saw a worsening sex ratio in Haryana. In 1991, not a single district recorded less than 800. In 2001, Haryana's well-known districts like Kurukshetra, Kaithal, Ambala, Sonepat, Rohtak, all recorded figures less than 800.

Gujarat, in 1991, enjoyed a sex ratio of 900 girls for every 1,000 boys, but the 2001 Census throws up a dismal picture. There is a sharp decline in a large number of its districts. Of the 20 districts in Gujarat, only eight recorded a child sex ratio of 900, the rest of the districts were very low. In fact in Rajkot and Mahesana, the situation is alarming and showed a ratio of just 798 girls per 1,000 boys.

In Himachal Pradesh too there is a drastic drop in the child sex ratio, especially in districts adjoining Punjab and Haryana. What was deemed a normal sex ratio of more than 950 in 1991, had dropped drastically in Himachal Pradesh, eight out of 12 districts being the worst. Most of the prosperous northern states have recorded more than a 50-point decline in the child sex ratio in the past 20 years.

In Rajasthan, more districts have recorded child sex ratios lower than 950, and it's slightly better amongst predominantly tribal populations. But even then, there has been a drop in child sex ratio especially in Chittorgarh and Udaipur. The child sex ratio has declined in Alwar, Sikar, Jaipur and Jhunjhunu districts. This could be attributed to the two-child norm pushed actively by the state government.

In 1991, Delhi's child sex ratio was lower than 950. Ten years later, the 2001 Census shows that almost all districts recorded a child sex ratio less than 900, with its more prosperous south-western part showing a decline from 904 girls in 1991 to 845 girls in 2001 and 871 girls in 2011.

In Maharashtra, in Jalgaon, Aurangabad, Beed, Solapur, Sangli and Kolhapur districts, the child sex ratio has gone from bad to worse. Maharashtra's eastern districts like Nagpur and Jalna also show a significant drop.

Of all the southern states that come up on the map of worsening child sex ratios, is Tamil Nadu. Little seems to have changed since 1991. Dharmapuri, Namkkal, Theni and Madurai districts had recorded a low child sex ratio in 1991. But the 2001 Census shows that the problem has spread to Tiruchi, Cuddalore and Vellore districts. In 1991, Salem had recorded the lowest child sex ratio at 830 girls which, the latest 2001 Census shows, has further declined to 826 girls per 1,000 boys.

Indian Census, it is important to understand that our sex ratio is defined as the number of females per 1,000 men, unlike the West where sex ratio is the complete opposite and defined as the number of males per 1,000 females. Like China, in India too masculinity is increasing. In India we have a poor civil birth registration system and most of our data are from hospitals where births have been registered. In India there are thousands of births that go unreported. So what we have is really biased data, not very reliable, but these are data constraints that we have to work with.

The phenomenon of declining sex ratio that showed up in Census 2001 is worst in Punjab, Haryana, Chandigarh, Delhi, Western Uttar Pradesh, Gujarat and Maharastra. This defies all demographic theories as these are prosperous states. When people live better, have better education and economic security, there will be less of a traditional bias against the girl-child; but in India, like China, it has only worsened the situation. Suppose like China, instead of just one, we had a two-child policy, then the Jats and Punjabis would ensure that they had two sons.

In India, there is an unholy alliance between tradition and technology. Tradition is marked by son-preference. Technology started in the 80's with amniocentesis, most readily available in Punjab, the state made most prosperous by the Green Revolution, and having a long tradition of son- preference. Today ultrasound is the sex-selective technology that is widespread in most prosperous states.

The reasons are easy to define – prosperity ensured better infrastructure, more machines and more doctors to perform the tests. People had money-power to pay for the technology and of course, as infrastructure improved, people could access the clinics easily. All this made foeticide rampant. If we look at the historical perspective of Punjab, where the sex ratio is the worst, the state has a long martial tradition, and women were seen as liabilities. Sons were preferred as they could carry on the martial tradition.

The new factor in Punjab is migration. Punjabis are the most eager to migrate to the West. The propensity to migrate is higher for young boys than for young girls. In Chandigarh, most young people are looking towards New Zealand for migration because that country is also agriculture-oriented.

In Haryana, the Jats have their own tradition of land ownership, so sons are preferred. It is a dismal situation. In the future, Punjabis will have to marry non-Punjabis, probably girls from Bihar and UP, which are demographically surplus-populated states.

The worst child sex-ratio was in Mahesana (762 girls per 1000 boys) in Gujrat, followed by Agra (772 girls per 1000 boys) in Uttar Pradesh, Modinagar (778) in Uttar Pradesh and English Bazaar (781) in West Bengal. Bally in West Bengal, had more girls (1185) per 1000 boys as did Nagaon (1043) in Assam and Tambaram (1019) in Tamil Nadu.

A normal gender ratio is 102-106 boys per 100 girls, which would be equivalent to 943-980 girls per 1000 boys, according to a report working on gender issues:

The child sex-ratio, which is based on the number of boys and girls between 0 and 6 years of age registered at the time of the census, shows whether sex-selection is prevalent in the country. A sex ratio less than the normal range of 943-980 girls per 1000 boys suggests discrimination against girls and the presence of female infanticide or female foeticide, which is sex-selection abortion of the foetus.

The sex ratio in India has been historically negative or in other words, unfavourable to females. Sex ratio reached its lowest in 1991 but since then has kept rising.

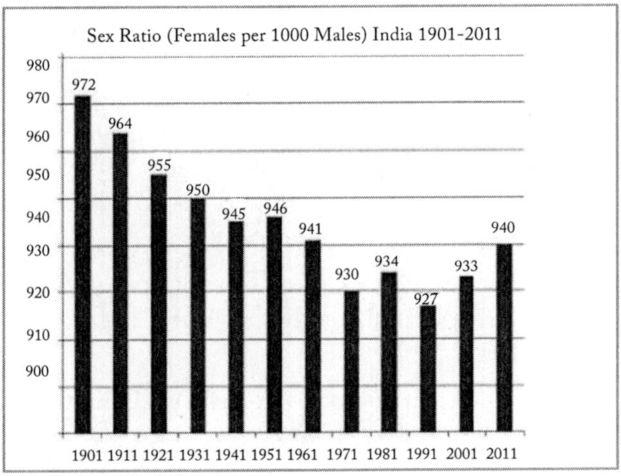

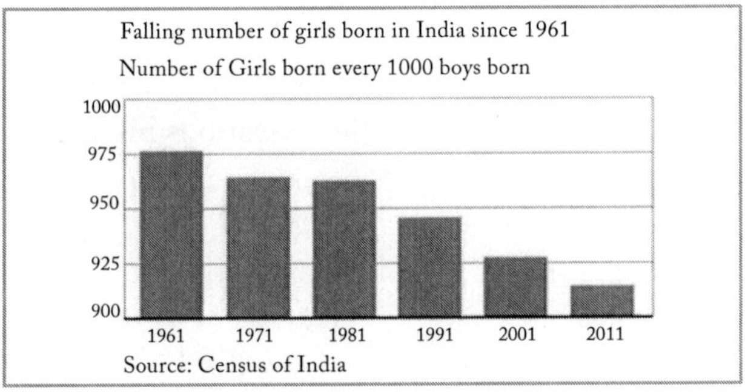

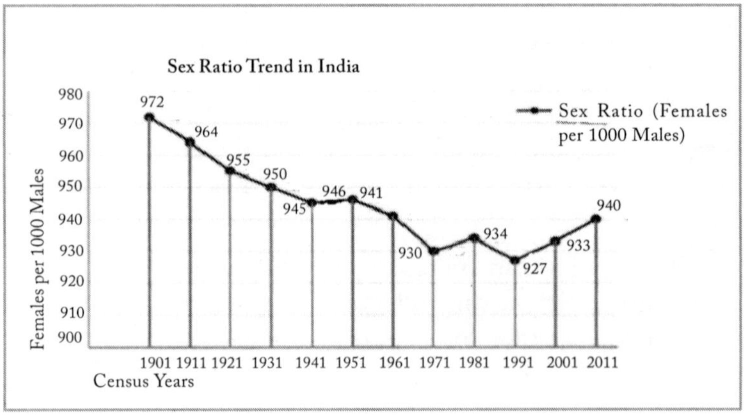

Rural and Urban Sex-ratio in India

As per 2011 India Census – 83,30,87,662 people live in rural India. 42,79,17,052 of them are males and 40,51,70,610 of are females. Female Sex-ratio in rural India is 947 women in every 1000 men. In Urban India the ratio drops to 926 women in every 1000 men.

Only 3 states and 1 Union Territory out of 27 states and 7 Union Territories in India has higher Rural and Urban female sex ratio than male.

States where rural female sex-ratio is higher than or equal to male are:

Kerala	–	1,077
Puduchhery	–	1,029
Chhatisgarh	–	1,002
Uttarakhand	–	1,000

States where urban female sex-ratio is higher than or equal to male are:

Kerala	–	1,091
Puduchhery	–	1,043
Manipur	–	1,038
Mizoram	–	1,000

Chandigarh has the lowest rural sex-ratio in India. Female sex-ratio in Chandigarh is only 691. NCT of Delhi also has very low both urban and rural female sex-ratio. It is 847 in rural and 867 in urban NCT of Delhi. Daman and Diu (UT) has the lowest urban female sex ratio of only 550 women in every 1000 men.

Data Highlights - Sex-Ratio

	2001	2011	Difference
Overall			
India	933	940	+ 7
Rural	946	947	+ 1
Urban	900	926	+26
0-6 years			
India	927	914	+13
Rural	934	919	-15
Urban	906	902	- 4

- The improvement in overall sex-ratio is largely in urban areas.
- Though the Urban Child sex-ratio is far worse than in the rural areas, the fall in child sex-ratio in rural areas is around 4 times that in urban areas. Infact the decline is more gradual in urban areas.
- There is a decline of 8-9 million children in rural areas, while in urban areas has shown increase of 3.9 million.

Growth of Rural and Urban Sex-ratio in India

After census in 2001 sex-ratio in urban India has grown quite impressively but it has almost no change in rural India. In 2001 census rural India has a female sex-ratio of 946 which increased by 1 and is now 947 females per 1000 males. Urban India had a sex-ratio of 900 at 2001 and it increased by 26 and reached 926 females per 1000 males in 2011.

Son-preference has spread even to south India. Social workers are saying the reason is patriarchy, or women having internaslised the value systems of men. The whole phenomenon is supply-driven rather than demand-driven and women feels they have a better self-image and status in society if they have sons.

In the population Census of 2011 it was revealed that the population ratio in 2011 is 940 females per 1000 of males. The sex ratio 2011 shows an upward trend from the census 2001 data. Census 2001 revealed that there were 933 females to that of 1000 males. Since decades India has seen a decrease in the sex ratio, but since the last two of the decades there has been in slight increase in the sex ratio.[6]

NOTES

1. Rudolph Joseph Rummel Buttresses: Professor emeritus of Political Science at the University of Hawaii. http://www.christiancadre.org/member_contrib/cp_infanticide.html. Adam Jones & Gendercide Watch 1999-2000.
2. http://www.iosworld.org/abortion-vs-female-foeticide.html
3. http://censusmp.nic.in
4. http://census2011.nic.in
5. m.timesofindia.com
6. Census of India

2

Female Foeticide:

Causes and Consequences

The main reason for the widespread female foeticide and the continuing prevalence of female infanticide in parts of India was the dowry system, which although long prohibited by law, continues to play a significant role in Indian society.

The general perception is that the cost of marriage and dowry has gone up and so daughters have become greater financial liabilities. The dowry system is invariably blamed. We are not convinced that dowry alone is the main cause of female foeticide. Families that are well-off and do not have to depend on dowry to augment their income are also opting for female foeticide. The real reason seems to be the high status of families with several sons and the low status of families with no sons. Another interesting factor for the preference for sons is that the prospect of migration of sons to, say the Gulf or western countries, is much higher for men than for women (except in special cases such as Kerala from where nurses go all over the world). In the eyes of the local community, a family with children abroad has a higher status and certainly a higher income level than non-migrant families. Globalisation is thus adding to the miseries of the girl child.

In short, there are numerous causes for the spread of female foeticide and it will be unscientific to believe that dowry alone is the cause, as is the general perception. Nevertheless, our perception during the fieldwork did reveal that people are aware of the upward swing in dowry demand and the rising cost of marriage. Greed has increased in our society and numerous TV channels and endless advertisements increase this greed further.

In the women's groups and organizations present, strongly condemned the Judgement of the Hon. Supreme Court in the matter of Appasaheb & Anr Vs. State of Maharashtra.[1] It was unanimously resolved that the Government of Maharashtra should immediately file a Review Petition in the Supreme Court for review of this Judgment.

The group expressed grave concern over the restrictive interpretation of dowry in the said judgment which nullifies the long struggle and campaign for reform in dowry laws by the women's movement. The group strongly felt that the judgement was regressive and set a precedent to allow dowry seekers and dowry death accused to go scot free.

The Commission forwarded the said resolution to the concerned government officials for necessary action. Therefore a meeting was also called on 12/02/07 by the Hon. Minister, Women and Child Development to discuss the ruling and steps to be initiated by the State Government. Hon. Minister directed the Home Department, to initiate necessary action with regard to filing of Review Petition.

Many women opted for female foeticide not because they were heartless but because they were genuinely concerned about the molestation and sexual harassment and, after marriage, exposed to the risk of bride burning and dowry death, in the unending demand for dowry from our emerging consumerist society (Lakshmi v. State of Tamil Nadu).[2] Lakshmi already had one daughter, so when she gave birth to a second girl, she killed her. For the three days of her second child's short life, Lakshmi admits, she refused to nurse her. To silence the infant's famished cries, the impoverished village woman squeezed the milky sap from an oleander shrub, mixed it with castor oil, and forced the poisonous portion down the newborn's throat. The baby bled from the nose, then died soon afterward. Female neighbors buried her in a small hole near Lakshmi's square thatched hut of sunbaked mud. They sympathized with Lakshmi, and in the same circumstances, some would probably have done what she did. For despite the risk of execution by hanging and about 16 months of a much-ballyhooed government scheme to assist families with daughters, in some hamlets of ... Tamil Nadu, murdering girls is still sometimes believed to be a wiser course than raising them. "A daughter is always liabilities. How can I bring up a second?" Lakshmi, 28, answered firmly when asked by a visitor how she could have taken her own child's life eight years ago. Instead of her suffering the way I do, I thought it was better to get rid of her.

This calls for a good look at gender issues in all their ramifications in our increasingly dysfunctional society. The another reasons for a girl child being considered a burden in Indian society -her marital value (The most immediate concern is the humbling sense a daughter's parents feel at her birth). As an infant and toddler, a girl is like fine china, parents take care that she turns out fair and beautiful. The 'fragile' and 'handle with care' item in a China shop is to remain a desirable bride for prospective patrons. She belongs to another family and not where she is born. By corollary, any mishandling by the trustees (parents/stewards) is likely to reduce the chances for her making it big in the marriage market. Marriage being central to life for women in most parts of India, parents are seized with a daughter's marriage. Her home, her identity and her prestige come through her marriage and in turn permeate the prestige for her natal family and the conjugal one. In being raised as a preferable bride, things are easier for her and her folks. It is in the cautious and careful vigil over a daughter, her sexuality and the training given to her to be affectionate, caring and responsible for her conjugal household members while being efficient and dexterous in household work, and if need be in taking up paid employment, that she is considered as having been raised with love and care.

In order that a daughter is desired as a marriage partner, her upbringing is accordingly fine tuned by the parents who then feel greatly relieved. It is a humbling experience to arrange a match for her, let alone the economic drain the marriage can be for her family. The sexuality of girls is closely guarded. She is likened to an earthen pot that should neither be dropped nor chipped. Unlike boys, girls are to be kept under a constant vigil. Wild girls are not good girls. This is an additional task to be performed with more resources and enhanced sense of responsibility. It is a resource the family has to provide for until a girl is married off. Such a vigil is necessitated more in urban areas and is increasingly needed in some rural areas and big towns as well. Sexual assault on unescorted girls and female children is on the rise, and is frequently reported in the media.

Simply put

1. Dowry system where parents of the bride have to pay the groom's family to marry their daughter. Higher the dowry, better the chances of a girl getting married. Of course, an unmarried girl is a blot on a family's honour, which leads me to my next point.
2. Misplaced archaic cultural (nonsense) of girls being the 'honour' of the family. Sadly, this is true for a majority of cultures around the world, but some take it seriously enough to resort to murderous acts for the sake of 'honour' that is driven by super-sized inflatable male chauvinist egos.
3. Girls don't propagate family name and neither does the family property stay in the same family.

Female foeticide is also rising because of the availability of technologies like ultrasonography and amniocentesis to determine the gender of foetuses at the request of the parents.

If the foetus is found to be a girl, it is aborted.

As a result, the government says around 10 million girls have been killed by their parents – either before or immediately after birth – over the past 20 years.

Experts warn that fewer women will spark a demographic crisis in many parts of country.

There is already this phenomenon all over the country where there is a lot of sexual violence and abuse against women and children across the country.

But when there are less women in the population and more men of the same age group, there is certainly going to be much more demand for women for marriage, for sex and this pressure will certainly increase violence against women.

CONSEQUENCES OF FEMALE FOETICIDE

Given the lower value placed on women in Indian society, prenatal sex determination with the intention of preventing female births must be viewed as a manifestation of violence against women, a violation of their human rights. Many women suffer from psychological trauma as a result of forcibly undergoing repeated abortions. More generally, demographers warn that in the next twenty years there will be a shortage of brides in the marriage market mainly because of the adverse juvenile sex ratio. But the preference for male children remains strong. For these families, modern medical technologies are within easy reach. Thus selective abortion and sex selection are becoming more common.

In rural areas, as the number of marriageable women declines, men would tend to marry younger women, leading to a rise in fertility rates and thus a high rate of population growth.

1. **Women's health:** There are women who have to undergo numerous abortions in hopes of getting a son at the risk of not being able to conceive again. They have even higher chances of being abused and abandoned by their husbands and families, once they cannot conceive and haven't even produced a son. Some women don't have the financial means to consult qualified physicians, so they settle for quacks who are available in plenty, and thus endanger their health immensely.

There are reports of these quacks prescribing testosterone to women who want a male child resulting in increase in cases of cancer among women and the birth of eunuchs. In addition to that, emotional and mental strain that a woman goes through is not considered important at all. She is left alone to suffer.

2. **Women being trafficked:** Stories of women being bought from the poor regions of the country for men who can't find themselves brides in the affluent parts affected by adverse sex-ratio are already making news. There are also news of women being bought and abandoned or sent to another man once they have produced a son. Long distance brides are being bought from a completely different culture and are forced to adjust to their new homes with new culture, new language, and far away from their families.

3. **Women being abused and sexually exploited:** Although it is invariably happening already, incidences of young girls (children) as well as older women being raped and forced into polygamy are to see a leap in numbers if the current trends of mass extinction of the female gender continues at the same pace.

4. **Suicide rates in women will increase:** Their psychological health will suffer. Their physical health will suffer. In short, the female gender is doomed if we don't do anything about fixing the problem we have at hand.

5. **Violence amongst men:** With a lack of proper family institution at home, men are bound to resort to aggressive means to expend their energy when they are not busy making money or beating women they bought because they couldn't give them sons in the first go.

Significant factors promoting Female Foeticide:

- The preference for boy in patriarchal society is so strong that many women choose to abort rather than give birth to a girl.
- Modern technology has helped a kill unwanted baby girls while still in the womb.
- There is also religious faith that parents want a son. Because only male children can perform the last rights for their parents.
- Women are forced to abort their female fetus owing to family pressure and the practice of dowry is responsible for this.

- Physical insecurity of women.

In India, there is an unholy alliance between tradition and technology. Tradition is marked by son-preference. Technology started in the 80's with amniocentesis, most readily available in Punjab, the state made most prosperous by the Green Revolution, and having a long tradition of son preference. Today ultrasound is the sex-selective technology that is widespread in most prosperous states.

NOTES

1. Appasaheb & Anr vs. State of Maharashtra, in Criminal Appeal No. 1613 of 2005.
2. AIR 2002.

3

Female Foeticide:
Remedial Measure

Step to Control Female Foeticide

This problem requires urgent attention of all parliamentarians, the government, the judiciary, media and public at large.

Steps to entirely eliminate female foeticide and its consequences can be divided into three categories.

- Preventing Sex Selection.
- Controlling the damage done due to sex selection.
- Mitigating the causes of sex selection.

Preventing Sex Selection: Ban Private Ultrasound Clinics

The PCPNDT Act has been in force since 1994 and that means that the law to regulate and prevent sex selection has been in place for more than 10 years. The law was amended in 2003 to include pre conception sex selection too. However even after 13 years of the law, the practice of sex selection continues unchecked. It is very easy to get sex selection test done on foetus at almost every one of the 30,000 clinics, if not all of them.

It could be argued that the implementation of law has been slow and ineffective and there is some truth in that. Indeed the Supreme Court judgment requiring rigorous punishment.

Indeed all that is happening is that government is now registering the murderers, criminals and perpetrators of genocide.

This is the first time in history of humanity, that a government of a civilized nation is spending more time in registering criminals, legitimizing murder and monitoring genocide rather than regulating criminals, preventing murder or stopping the genocide.

There is no denying that the PCPNDT Act is not being implemented effectively enough. But this debate takes away from the fact that perhaps the law itself may be faulty. And indeed the PCPNDT Act is totally, entirely and completely faulty.

Now if a few clinics - say a thousand or a little more of the 30,000 ultrasound clinics were indulging in sex selection tests, it could have been argued that law is not being implemented effectively. But almost all the 30,000 clinics are violating the law to some extent. After all the law does not merely prohibit sex selection tests, but allows use of pre natal diagnostic tests only for certain medical conditions. But almost every clinic openly uses ultrasound test for spurious, specious reason called foetal well being. This itself is violation of law and calls for shutting down these 30,000 clinics.

Actually there is no reason for these 30,000 clinics to exist in first place. Ultrasound technology is rarely required for reasons other than pre natal diagnostic technique. Very rarely is ultrasound required for examination of kidney, liver or abdomen. Most of the usage of ultrasound technology is restricted to examination of pregnant women.

Now almost all of pregnancy cases do not require ultrasound examination. It is in very rare case of pregnancy that ultrasound examination is mandatory and adds value. Indeed the PCPNDT Act specifies only few conditions for which ultrasound prenatal diagnostic technique may be resorted too. But most of the ultrasound clinics routinely carry out ultrasound examination, thus totally, entirely and completely violating the law.

Indeed if ultrasound examination were to be restricted to only for the reasons specified in PCPNDT Act, a very small fraction of pregnancy cases would require ultrasound examination.

And India would be able to provide a market for at most a thousand or a little more ultrasound machines.

However it is the clear violation of PCPNDT Act and the routine usage of ultrasound examination for prenatal diagnosis that has led to mushrooming of ultrasound clinics. Indeed if the PCPNDT Act were to be strictly implemented, not just to prevent sex selection test, but to ensure that ultrasound technology is used only for medical reasons specified in the act, then each and every one of the ultrasound clinic would be found to be violating law and thus effectively indulging in crime.

Now it is very clear that firstly that almost all the 30,000 clinics, even those not indulging in sex determination tests, are violating the PCPNDT act by routinely engaging in prenatal diagnostic technique for reasons not mentioned in the PCPNDT Act. Secondly, if one were to restrict pre natal diagnostic techniques only for reasons specified in the PCPNDT Act, India would require only a thousand or little more ultrasound machine clinics and not 30,000 clinics.

Hence the PCPNDT Act must be amended to entirely ban private ultrasound clinics. India does not need 30,000 ultrasound clinics. India may need a thousand or more ultrasound machines and these can be housed within government hospitals, health centers and thus carefully regulated.

There is bound to be huge resistance to this move to entirely ban private ultrasound clinics. But then the response of the government is obvious. Firstly most, if not all ultrasound clinics are carrying out sex determination tests. And each and every one of them is violating the PCPNDT Act by carrying out routine prenatal diagnostic tests for reasons not specified in PCPNDT Act.

Thus if each and every of the 30,000 clinics is a criminal clinic, this calls for complete banning of private ultrasound clinics. The government must amend the PCPNDT Act to completely ban private ultrasound clinics.

Implement the PCPNDT Act stringently, rigorously and closely

The government's effort at implementing the PCPNDT Act makes mockery of the Act. There is a PCPNDT cell in the ministry of health and family welfare. However this has staff strength of less than 10. Further, the PCPNDT cell is so impoverished that it does not even have a STD phone; leave alone technology required to closely implement the law.

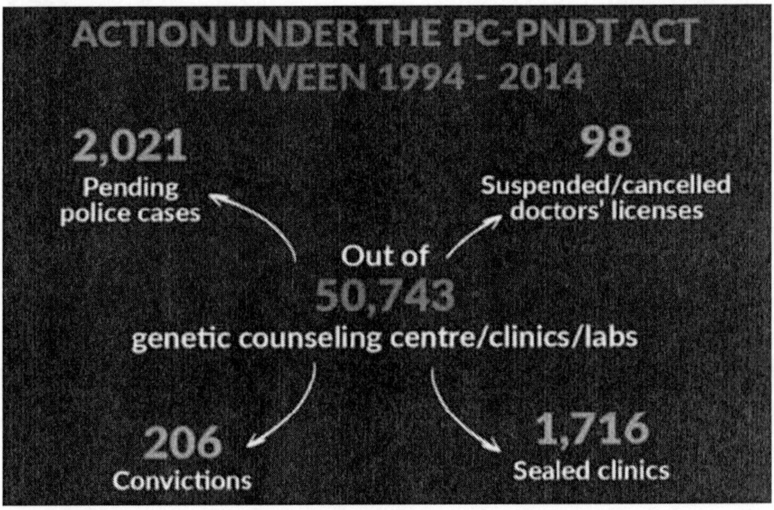

Now the PCPNDT Act can be implemented either by carrying out "decoy operations" or by examining the Form F records. Both these means must be resorted to identify culprit clinics violating the PCPNDT Act.

However firstly the PCPNDT cell in the union ministry must be strengthened. The staff strength of PCPNDT cell should be immediately increased to 1000, with 600 of the staff deputed to each of the 600 districts in India. Each of these 600 PCPNDT officers in every district will be required to carry out at least one sting operation every week. The modus operandi of sting operation is simple - take a pregnant woman to a clinic with accompanying person carrying a recording (audio/video) device. In case the doctor reveals the sex of the foetus, we have evidence. Now the chief medical officer of the district would be required to seize the equipment and file case against the doctor.

Currently the PCPNDT cell under union ministry does not even carry out single sting operation. But in case 600 officers are required to carry out one sting operation every week, the ministry would succeed in carrying out 30,000 "sting operations" in a year. Further the PCPNDT officer in each district has to work closely with the chief medical officer, or appropriate district authority to ensure that PCPNDT Act is closely implemented.

Not only would the PCPNDT officer carry out sting operation, but also carry out medical audit on all the clinics examining the Form F and other records. Now if the Form F has glaring flaws such as mentioning same name often, or many other discrepancies, clearly that calls for seizing the equipment and filing case. But more than that, even if the clinic is carrying out prenatal diagnostic technique for routine examination for foetal well being and for reasons not specified in the PCPNDT Act, that itself calls for seizing the equipment and filing case against the doctor.

In addition to 600 PCPNDT officers deputed to each district, 300 officers from PCPNDT cell would tour various districts and carry out random medical audit on each clinic - say an audit of 2 clinics every week. Further they would monitor the implementation of PCPNDT act in each and every district in India from the centre.

There is an urgent need to increase the staff strength of the PCPNDT cell to 1000, of which 600 officers are deputed to each district and 300 monitor various districts from the centre. The budget for the PCPNDT cell should be increased to Rs. 200 crore to ensure effective implementation of PCPNDT Act.

Ideally the PCPNDT Act needs to be amended to entirely ban private ultrasound clinics. But till such time that private ultrasound clinics are entirely banned, an interim measure would be ensuring that PCPNDT Act is effectively implemented. And that cannot be effective by mere modifying rhetoric from the Health Minister, but requires substantial resources allocated to PCPNDT cell – Rs. 200 crores annually and a staff of 1000 officers.

Participation by Government, Civil Society and Media

In a country like India, a caring and protective environment for girl children does not develop easily. Failure to ensure protection of the girl children entails their promotion, prevention and rehabilitation. However, many initiatives have been developed and legislation exits in theory to protect girl children.

Some exemplary district administrations have taken a lead in combating this problem. In a district of Andhra Pradesh, a system of methodically auditing all scan centers in the district was introduced. Details of the scans, the personal information of the families were noted and authorities were able to follow up on the cases until the birth of the children. The district handed out 361 notices, suspended 91 registrations, and seized 54 scan machines. Three suppliers were prosecuted for distributing the pre-natal diagnostic machines without proper registration.

In Haryana, the 'Ladli' scheme for the girl child was drawn up by the State Government to provide incentives to the family. Under this scheme, a sum of Rs. 5000/- per annum for five years is paid to couples giving birth to a second girl child (Rs. 2,500/- for each of the two girl children). This money is invested in Kisan Vikas Patras in the joint names of the second girl child and the mother. In case the mother is not alive, then this money is transferred to a joint account of the second girl child and father.

Non-governmental organisations (NGOs) have also organized campaigns, rallies and programs to raise awareness about female foeticide around the country. They work with various stakeholders including other NGOs, governmental agencies, media, medical professionals, opinion makers, religious leaders, role models, youth icons and the communities.

Media highlighted the problem through investigative reports and articles, they launched widespread awareness campaigns in the form of video spots on national and private television stations.

GOVERNMENT ROLE

NGOs started to become aware of this mushrooming technology in mid 80s, and Maharashtra enacted law in 1988, banning use of technology for sex determination. In 1994, the Union Government of India enacted PCPNDT that made revealing sex of the foetus a criminal offence. The PCPNDT Act, while by no means entirely perfect, would have contained the sex selection industry. However its implementation has been very lenient, careless and ineffective.

While Supreme Court has passed orders on improving the implementation of Act in response to PIL filed by Cehat in May 2000, the implementation of the law continues to be very feeble. The only improvement has been that most ultrasound clinics are now registered, but this has not prevented them from continuing with sex determination tests.

Indeed with 30,000 registered ultrasound clinics spread all over the nation and a sex-ratio at birth that hovers around 900 females per 1000 males, indicating sex selective abortion to the tune of a million per year, it comes as a shock that there have been only 300 prosecutions (mainly for non registration) and only one conviction. The very fact that almost a million sex selective abortions take place in India annually points to the fact that atleast 10,000 to 20,000 or more of the 30,000 clinics are either openly or covertly carrying out sex determination tests.

But the implementation of PCPNDT Act is so weak, that there is nothing apart from the conscience of the doctor to prevent sex selection tests from being carried out. The PCPNDT cell in the ministry of health and family welfare has staff strength of less than 10 individuals, whereas for a problem of this magnitude it needs to be few hundred.

Further the chief medical officer or the district magistrate of each district who is supposed to monitor the implementation of PCPNDT Act in that district are burdened with hundred other responsibilities, that makes it impossible to devote any time or attention to regulating the ultrasound clinics through PCPNDT Act.

Thus there is a PCPNDT Act, which requires each doctor to maintain documents (Form F) regarding every patient being treated with the ultrasound machine for pre natal diagnostic techniques. Again it allows the usage of ultrasound machine only for certain reasons and not for every pregnant woman. And revealing sex is clearly banned. However, in practice almost no doctor maintains documents, thus violating the law. Further ultrasound diagnosis is now prescribed routinely for foetal well being thus violating the law. Again and this has to be established through a decoy operation, sex determination tests are covertly practiced in almost 10,000 to 20,000 or more of these ultrasound clinics.

With the sex ratio in the Capital on the decline, Delhi government is set to bring about a legislation providing for stringent auditing of the records of ultrasound clinics.

"The government will tackle this problem (female foeticide) by not only carrying out a comprehensive public awareness campaign but by also bringing about effective legislation to provide a fool-proof system of auditing records of ultrasound diagnostic clinics,"

"If all the women in our families unite to fight against the sin of female foeticide, nobody will be able to stop us from overcoming this evil".

The Government also inaugurated a website set up by Delhi Commission for Women (DCW) to facilitate on-line registration of complaints.

Advocating the induction of more women constables in the police so that women feel more comfortable in registering their complaints.

The chief minister also announced short-term courses on women's studies to be conducted by Delhi University as well as a scheme to promote cooperative societies run by underprivileged women:

1. Parliament must devote entire day to discussing Female Foeticide;
2. Parliament must amend PCPNDT Act to ban private Ultrasound Clinics;
3. Dowry Prohibition Act and Marriage Expenses Control Act must be implemented rigorously by creating a special ministry under union government for this purpose with a budget of Rs. 600 crore;
4. A complete National Aids Control Organisation (NACO) like cell should be created to implement PCPNDT Act with funds of Rs. 100 crores annually and staff strength of at least 1000.

Genocide in India is going unreported. Female Foeticide is a well-known fact. But the extent of it calls for its classification as a veritable genocide. For instance the 2001 Census figures point to a sex ratio for 0-6 age group of around 927 females per 1000 males. The sex ratio at birth has further worsened by 2002-03 by some rough estimates from civil registration of births to almost 882 females per 1000 males. Assuming an average of 900 females per 1000 males, this points out that almost 10 per cent of females are missing.

The sex ratio is worse in some states such as Punjab, Haryana, Rajasthan, Gujarat, Delhi and Maharashtra.

State	Sex Ratio in 0-6 age group-Census 2001		Sex Ratio in 0-6 age group-Census 2011	
	Rural	Urban	Rural	Urban
1	2	3	4	5
Punjab	866	789	907	875
Haryana	884	809	882	873
Rajasthan	909	886	933	914
Delhi	917	866	852	868

contd...

1	2	3	4	5
Uttar Pradesh	928	880	918	894
Bihar	949	924	921	895
West Bengal	955	948	953	944
Orissa	949	927	989	932
Madhya Pradesh	960	941	936	918
Gujarat	908	827	949	880
Maharashtra	930	908	952	903
Andhra Pradesh	962	958	996	987
Karnataka	951	939	979	963
Kerala	958	951	1078	1091
Tamil Nadu	951	951	993	1000
India	934	905	949	929

Source : Census 2001, 2011

The above table points to an alarming situation. Just imagine a state like Haryana where sex ratio at birth is just around 873 per thousand – clearly almost 13 per cent of female foetuses are selectively aborted. The Punjab situation is equally threatening. Gujarat is especially bad with sex ratio very low at a mere 880 in urban areas.

Policy Framework

National Plan of Action exclusively for the girl child (1991-2000) was formulated in 1992 for the "Survival, Protection and Development of the Girl Children". The Plan recognized the rights of the girl child to equal opportunity, to be free from hunger, illiteracy, ignorance and exploitation. Towards ensuring survival of the girl child, the objectives are to:

1. Prevent cases of female foeticide and infanticide and ban the practice of amniocentesis for sex determination;
2. End gender disparity in infant mortality rate; eliminate gender disparities in feeding practices, expand nutritional interventions to reduce severe malnourishment by half and provide supplementary nutrition to adolescent girls in need;

3. Reduce deaths due to diarrhoea by 50 per cent among girl children under 5 years and ensure immunization against all forms of serious illnesses; and
4. Provide safe drinking water and ensure access to fodder and drinking water nearer home.

The launching of the *Balika Samriddhi Yojana* in 1997 is a major initiative of Government to raise the overall status of the girl child. It intends to change family and community attitudes towards her and her mother. Under this scheme about 25 lakh girl children born every year in families below the poverty line are to be benefited. The first component of the scheme, which has already been launched, is to provide Rs. 500 as a post-delivery grant to the mother of the girl child as a symbolic gift from Government. The other components proposed under the scheme are provision of annual scholarships to the beneficiaries when they go to school and assistance for taking upon income generating activity when they attain the age of maturity.

Besides having specific legislation and policy proclamations to deal with this menace, the precipitating factors such as dowry, poverty, and woman's economic dependence etc., leading to the problem of foeticide and infanticide have been addressed by enacting various legislations as:

- Dowry Prohibition Act, 1961 (Amended in 1986);
- Hindu Marriage Act, 1955;
- Hindu Adoption and Maintenance Act, 1956;
- Immoral Traffic Prevention Act, 1986;
- Equal Remuneration Act, 1976 etc.

These and various other legislations and policy proclamations intend to bring about women's economic and social empowerment to the maximum.

Grappling with incidents of crime against women, the Government of different states has decided to set up a women's help cell in every district of the state official. The move intends to check various manifestations of violence against women, particularly dowry harassment and female foeticide.

All India Women's Helpline No. is 1090. It should help in places where there are no accessible or working helplines.

In UP, cases of crime against women are reported particularly from its western districts including Moradabad, Muzaffarnagar and Meerut.

The average sex ratio of the state is 898 females per 1,000 males. However, the ratio in several districts including Hardoi, Shahjahanpur, Badaun and Etah is extremely poor. In these districts there are less than 850 females per 1,000 males.

This is believed to be an indicator of increasing incidence of female foeticide in the state. The government had also ordered a crackdown on ultrasound centres across the state, especially in western Uttar Pradesh.

DOCTOR'S ROLE

Doctors abetting female foeticide will be debarred from practice.

In a significant move against female foeticide, the Tamil Nadu Medical Council (TNMC) declared that it would come down heavily against doctors abetting in discriminatory abortions of girls, and debar them from practice if necessary.

Role of doctors in halting the declining sex ratio and implementation of the Prenatal Diagnostics Tests Prevention Act, indulged in some severe doctor-bashing, holding the medical fraternity "squarely responsible" for the high incidence of female foeticide in the country.

Haryana court sentenced a woman doctor and a couple to three-year imprisonment for female foeticide.

Judicial Magistrate Satish Kumar awarded the sentence to Reshma Yadav, proprietor of Janseva Hospital, Anil Kumar and his wife Sunita, residents of Begpur village in Narnaul, 310 km from here. The Court found them guilty under the Pre-Natal Diagnostic Techniques (Regulation and Prevention of Misuse) Act.

A team of the State Health Department had detected a case of female foeticide during a raid at the hospital on June 18, 2008, and registered cases against Dr. Yadav and the couple.[1]

Doctors were helping parents "kill girls before birth" through abortions after determining the sex of the unborn child using scanning devices.

The TNMC president, M. Balasubramanian, said the medical fraternity should not dismiss the accusations lightly. On their entrance to the profession, doctors were clearly instructed in a booklet on medical ethics that female foeticide was a heinous crime.

He invited individuals and community organisations to bring to the notice of the council, scan centres and doctors indulging in sex determination and eventual abortions. If convinced, the council would constitute a disciplinary committee to enquire into the complaint and issue warnings, temporary cancel the registration or even permanently debar doctors from practice.

The TNMC is the registering authority for medical practitioners.

The uncontrolled mushrooming of scan centres in Tamil Nadu. "In villages, whether or not there are good medical centres to take care of diseases such as tuberculosis, there is at least one scan centre."

The scans were necessary to detect likely birth defects, "When there are only 0.1 per cent birth defects in Tamil Nadu, why should it have 1,764 scan centres if not for female foeticide? This is murder."

The Chairperson of the Tamil Nadu State Commission for Women, V. Vasanthi Devi, said amendments to the PCPNDT Act had several positive aspects, and the Indian Medical Association and the Medical Council of India should be proactive in incorporating it as part of their rules.

The Director of Access, Mina Swaminathan, said doctors should not recommend scanning for pregnant women unless there was a medical necessity, and insisted that future technology for sex determination be available only in government hospitals.

Chandigarh, The Haryana Medical Council has cancelled the registration of a doctor for five years for being convicted by a court for violation of Pre-natal Diagnostic Technique Act. Registrar of Medical Council, Haryana, Dr K.K. Kapoor said the Medical Council notice states: "The Medical Council has decided to remove the name of Dr M.P. Kamboj, registration no. HN 2740, from the register of registered medical practitioners maintained by the Haryana Medical Council under Section 11 of the Punjab Medical Registration Act, 1916, for being convicted by Chief Judicial Magistrate, Hisar, as pronounced on January 10, 2008, for committing offence under Section 4(3) and 5(1) (b) read with Rule 9 of PCPNDT Act and rules which are punishable under Section 23(2) of the Act and his name has accordingly been removed from the register with effect from January 10, 2008 (afternoon) for a period of five years."

Dr Kapoor said charges have also been framed against another doctor, N.C. Bansal of Hisar, for violation of the PNDT Act.[2]

Director General, Health Services, Dr Avinash Sharma said strict action would go a long way in checking malpractices in the health system. He said Haryana was the first state in the country to have recorded five convictions for sex determination under the PNDT Act and was the only state in the country having the highest number of convictions for sex determination.

Licence of Delhi Gynaecolgist suspended after BBC report[3]

Licence of Indian gynaecologist was suspended after a BBC report into female foeticide. Dr Mangala Telang a Delhi based gynaecologist was filmed offering an illegal ultrasound scan, although she denied any wrongdoing. Her two Delhi clinics have been shut down. The BBC had sent a British couple to one of Dr Telang's clinics in Delhi after hearing that her clinic would offer ultrasound scans to determine the sex of a baby. In the BBC film,

Dr Telang was caught agreeing to perform the scan to determine whether the woman's unborn child was a boy or a girl - even though a sign in the waiting room clearly said the practice was illegal. As per the story on BBC web site Dr Telang had told the BBC team she could recommend someone to carry out an abortion if the foetus was female. Despite India's strict laws to prevent female foeticide, prosecutions remain rare.

ROLE OF NGOS

NGO to Campaign against Female Foeticide

A city-based NGO will take out rallies, hold street plays, protests marches and community discourses in Haryana with one message – do not kill unborn daughters. The state has one of the worst sex ratios in the country, 819 women per 1,000 men.

The two-year campaign fight against female foeticide will be launched by the Centre for Social Research (CSR) as a pilot project in two districts of Haryana, Kurukshetra and Ambala, which have the lowest sex ratio – 770 females and 784 females per 1,000 males respectively.

"Delhi, Punjab and Haryana are some of the highly prosperous states in the country. Ironically, these are the very same states which have a bad reputation for killing the unborn daughters in the womb.

"Haryana's districts like Kurukshetra, Kaithal, Ambala, Sonepat, Rohtak recorded figures of less than 800 girls per 1,000 boys. Sonepat has 783 girls per 1,000 boys and Rohtak 796 girls per 1,000. The numbers show that there is no sign of the trend reversing.

Haryana is the second place after Delhi where the NGO has launched such a campaign.

"Female foeticide is fast emerging as a big problem in our country. Income and wealth, usually taken as symbols of prosperity and development, have not led to a change in the social mindset of the people. It is now clear that the prosperous areas of the city are not immune to the trend of female foeticide.

Survey by NGO reveals that Chembur Clinics in Mumbai flout Sex tests

A survey of 40 ultra-sound clinics in Chembur by Laadli Alliance, a group of 10 NGOs has revealed shocking revelations. Not one of the 40 clinics here follows the rules prescribed in the Pre-conception and Pre-natal Diagnostic Techniques (Prohibition of Sex Selection) Act 1994 (PCPNDT Act), aimed at curbing female foeticide.

Mumbai's sex ratio is 898 girls per 1000 boys. Sex discrimination and female foeticide are issues that Mumbai needs to tackle on a war footing. The report is being sent to public health department, family welfare department and National PCPNDT Cell, of the Brihan Mumbai Municipal Corporation (BMC), demanding strict action against the clinics.

"Four teams, armed with authorisation letters from the BMC, surveyed 47 sonography clinics in Mumbai (West) Ward between July 18 and August 8 2007. Seven of the clinics were non-operational, the remaining 40 were found to be flouting various rules of the PCPNDT Act. Shockingly many doctors claimed that they were not even aware of the Act.

Initiatives Developed by NGOs and Governments

Many initiatives have been developed by non-government actors to protect more effectively the girl child. Girl discrimination can be gradually challenged. Negative gender-based norms and practices may be transformed through educational, social, legal and other processes that promote equality of girls and boys. Girl children need both preventive and corrective protection.

Government, international and regional agencies as NGO's could commit themselves to address patriarchy, son preference as well as negative stereotypes and practices, and to empower girls to realize their human rights. Effective implementation of the existing legislation, existence of penalty and punishment, legal and policy reforms, advocating for women and gender-sensitive data collection, development of projects that improve women's health and expand their choices in life are also necessary.

It is essential to give young girls adequate information, guidance on reproductive and sexual health and to provide them with necessary services to protect their health and development. Educating girls and providing them with skills development and training is a powerful level for their empowerment, as well as for reducing poverty. Education can translate into economic opportunities for women and their families. Girls who are educated are also likely to marry later and to have smaller, healthier families. Education helps girls to know their rights and claim them, for themselves and their families. A girl's life will be determined by how the mother is living and whether her rights are respected. If a mother, who was lucky enough to survive the birth of her children, has no education, labours long hours, is denied the right to own property and control resources, she will be condemned to a life of poverty making it difficult for her to provide a better life for her child. It is consequently of utter importance to address early the root factors of gender inequality. Gender equality may help to promote the active participation of girls as agents of change in their own lives, families, communities and societies and to overcome gradually poverty.

It is also essential to educate boys at school to respect, consider and even protect girls and women.

Some initiatives developed by NGOs and governments to fight against female foeticide and girl infanticide include:

- Mass campaigns and rallies for awareness;
- Workshops, lectures, video spots, advertising and publication of articles;
- Piloting of conditional cash transfer schemes to support the survival and development of the girl child;
- Universal birth registration;

- Registration of pregnancies;
- Registration of ultrasound clinics;
- Collecting data on the status of the girl child, on still-born sex ratios and aborted foetuses sex ratio;
- Constitution of vigil communities/task forces.

It is also necessary to consider what happens to girl children rescued or recovered from exploitation or abuse. Mechanisms for their recovery as well as their rehabilitation need to be developed. Existing schemes tend to emphasize restoration to the family setting however in many cases - for a girl child rescued from early marriage, sale rape, or a child recovered from a hostility/conflict zone – the family of origin may not be the best option available for re-location. Mechanisms are essential to provide shelter, counseling, possibility of foster or alternate placement, re-entry into schooling or development programs and for any prosecution of offenders.

Child protection services at the local level must exercise special vigilance on the situation of girl children in every community. They will need to devise special needed approaches to serve girl children at all stages of childhood.

NOTES

1. AIR, 2008, State of Haryana
2. AIR, 2008, State of Haryana
3. BBC News 5th Dec., 2007

4

Judicial Responses and Role of Judiciary

The judiciary in India will observe 2007 as the Awareness Year of Female Foeticide and will deal in a strict manner with those responsible for this crime, former Chief Justice Y.K. Sabharwal had declared while delivering his presidential address at a state-level seminar on 'Eradication of Female Foeticide', jointly organised by the Punjab Department of Health and Family Welfare and Punjab Legal Services Authority.

The law can play an important role in checking this menace of female foeticide, he added. Warning the medical fraternity, he said there ought to be stricter control over clinics that offer to identify the sex of a foetus and a stronger check on abortions to ensure that these are not performed for the wrong reasons. Doctors must also be sensitised and strong punitive measures must be taken against those who violate the law.

It will be interesting to investigate how the judiciary at different levels exhortations of the highest in the judiciary. The case in this instance cited below refers to Morena in Madhya Pradesh, one of the very few districts in the country where this issue has been vigorously persuade and a game of snakes and ladder is being played out.

A team of district officials did a door-to-door survey in a village and came up with an alarmingly adverse child sex ratio. When this was discussed with the villagers in the evening, they not only accepted the figures but also openly disclosed the fact of sex determination through sonography and termination thereafter in case of a female child and also the names of the nursing homes they visited for sex determination.

Discussions were undertaken with the medical fraternity in the district with a view to discouraging sex determination and so that the district authorities would not permit this heinous practice. However, there was no visible change in the attitude of doctors, therefore the records of nine centres registered under the Act were seized.

These records were scrutinised and it was observed that non-compliance with the maintenance of mandated records was very common at the registered centres. The laxity was more prominent with the Form-F requirement. Through this form only the following vital information can be obtained:

(1) Number of children with sex of each child.

(2) Purpose for which ultrasound was done during pregnancy.

(3) Result of ultrasonography - if any abnormality detected.

(4) Was the maternal terminal of pregnancy come into force in 1971 advised/conducted - Date on which MTP carried out.

(5) Declaration of doctor that while conducting ultrasonography, he has neither detected nor disclosed the sex of her foetus to anybody in any manner.

(6) Declaration of the pregnant woman that by undergoing ultrasonography, she does not want to know the sex of the foetus.

After a scrutiny of the records, the appropriate authority, the chief medical and health officer, issued show cause notices and finally cancelled seven registrations. In the instance of one centre, which was operating two machines in two different locations with one registration, a case was submitted before the chief judicial magistrate. No discernible result in this case could be seen till date.

All the seven nursing homes/ultrasound centres appealed against the cancellation in the month of June 2005, much after the prescribed duration. The State Appellant Authority condoned the delay in all the cases, and decided all the seven cases on the same date of June 10, 2005 giving almost identical reasons for accepting the appeal and quashing the order of the appropriate authority even though the merits and grounds were different in all the cases.

The Appellate Authority, while admitting that Form 'F[1] was not maintained by these centres and also that records for the last two years were not maintained, observed that 'although there is no clear evidence of maintaining all the prescribed records as envisaged under section 4(3) and rule 9 of the Act, but looking to the records made available, it does not amount to a gross irregularity to cancel the registration of the appellant.

This order of the state Appellate Authority was challenged by two NGOs namely '*Prayatn*' and '*Dharti Gram Utthan*, which work in Morena on this issue, by filing a Public Interest Litigation (PIL) in the high court of Madhya Pradesh's Gwalior bench.

The petitioners argued that the erroneously called such violation a 'mere irregularity[1] and felt that if the reasoning given by the State Appellate Authority were accepted, it would result in total non-implementation of the Act and rules against female foeticide resulting in a further decline of the sex ratio in Morena district.

This petition was admitted for final hearing and the operation of the impugned order of the state Appellate Authority was stayed. In the meantime, the court directed that all the Chief Medical and Health Officers (CMHOs) and District Collectors of Morena, Guna, Shivpuri, Ashok Nagar, Vidisha, Datia, Sheopur, Bhind and Gwalior make a survey and inspect all the nursing homes as well as the laboratories and centres where the ultrasound machines were being used.

They would have to verify that in such nursing homes and the laboratories/centres appropriate measures were being adopted to restrain, avoid and prohibit the sex determination and sex selection process. They would have to survey all the towns of the district where these machines were being used and submit the report before the court. They would also have to suggest the effective measures to prohibit and prevent such kind of determination.

The state was also directed to seek a report from the Morena collector about the status of involvement of respondents whose licenses were cancelled, whether they were involved in the cases of sex selection and sex determination at the pre-conception and pre-natal stage.

On Dec 13, 2006, five respondents filed applications and contended that they had applied for permission to run the ultrasound machines, as they were not involved in pre-natal sex determination, although the CMHO of Morena submitted that the owners of these machines were not furnishing proper information in proper format.

The Court directed that in view of this fact, the respondents would be permitted to run their ultrasound machines but made it clear that they would have to furnish regular information as required under PCPNDT Act of 1994 and the rules framed there under. It said the competent authority would also have the liberty to supervise and make proper checks of the machines and take action in case any breach was found against them as per the Act and the Rules.

Reports reveal that baby girls are neglected, malnourished or even killed at birth. Evidence suggests that sex selecting clinics and the abortion of girls are still wide spread. Tougher legislation have made it possible for the authorities to crack down staging raids on pre-natal clinics to check records and look for evidence of illegal sex selection. Officials admit that it is hard to find evidence. Pre-natal scans to check for abnormalities are legal and it can be impossible to prove that a doctor has infact used one to reveal baby's sex. The recent study has reported that India has lost 10 million girls over the last two decades. After the enactment of the PCPNDT act in 1994, in the year 2006 there was first conviction.

Where a doctor and a lab technician were sentenced to two year of imprisonment under the act.

Public Interest Litigation was also file in Supreme Court by concerned health activists. Centre for Enquiry into Health and Allied Themes (CEHAT) v. Union of India.[1]

In response to the petition, the court issued notices to the Central and State Governments to file replies to Central Supervisory Board, State Governments under the administrations and to appoint appropriate authorities at district and sub-district level. Directions stated that the list of the members appointed should be published in the print and electronic media. Appropriate authorities were further directed to send a quarterly report to the central supervisory board, public awareness against the practice of pre-natal sex determination.

Supreme Court directed state governments to take further steps to enforce the law. Department of family welfare was directed to file an affidavit indicating the status of actions taken. Supreme Court directed 9 companies to supply the information of the machines sold to various clinics in the last 5 years. Details of about 11,200 machines from all these companies and fed into a common data base. Addresses received from the manufacturers were also sent to concerned states and to launch prosecution against those bodies using ultrasound machines that had filed to get themselves registered under the act. The court directed that the ultrasound machines/scanners be sealed and seized if they were being used without registration. Three associations viz., The Indian Medical Association (IMA), Indian Radiologist Association (IRA), and the Federation of Obstetricians and Gynecologists Societies of India (FOGSI) were asked to furnish details of members using these machines. Since the supreme court directive 99 cases were registered and in 232 cases ultrasound machines, other equipment and records were seized. Today there is an estimated 25000 ultrasound machines in the country, of these 15000 have been registered. State governments have communicated to the central government in writing the according to official reports received, they are satisfied that sex determination services are no longer being provided in their respective states.

However, it is widely believed that while these services are no longer openly available their clandestine availability and utilization continues all over the country. The observation of the National Inspection and Monitoring Commission confirm this situation and endorse the need for stricter enforcement of laws.

National Framework

The Constitution of India guarantees:

- Equality before the law and equal protection of laws to each and every person in the country (Article 14).
- Prohibits discrimination on grounds of race, caste, sex, descent, place of birth or residence (Article 15).
- Prohibits discrimination on grounds of race, caste, sex or place of birth in any public employment (Article 16).

The National Charter for Children (link, part Instruments/ National level/National policies) refers also especially to the protection of the girl child.

The main law for prosecuting persons who are engaging in sex selective abortion is the Pre-Natal Diagnostic Techniques (Regulation and Prevention of Misuse) Act, 1994. This Act provides for the prevention of misuse of such techniques for the purpose of prenatal sex determination leading to female foeticide.

- It prohibits misuse and advertisement of pre-natal diagnostic techniques for determination of sex of foetus, leading to female foeticide.
- It permits and regulates the use of pre-natal diagnostic techniques for detection of specific genetic abnormalities or disorders and use of such techniques only under certain conditions and only by the registered institutions.
- It gives punishment for violation of the provisions given in the Act.
- The complaint made by any person should be first given to the appropriate authority with the notice of not less than thirty days

for proper action and with the intention to make a complaint to the court.

On 17 January 2003, India amended its Pre-natal Diagnostic Techniques (Regulation and Prevention of Misuse) Act, 1994 that was renamed Pre-Conception and Pre-Natal Diagnostic Techniques Act (PCPNDT) of 2003.

The 2003 amendment is designed to strengthen the provisions of the previous Act.

- It prohibits the causing of sex selection before or after conception;
- It enlarges the scope of procedures and tests that are prohibited and categories of clinics and laboratories that are subject to the provisions of the Act;
- It broads advertising prohibitions;
- It prohibits the sale of any ultrasound machine or imaging machine or scanner or any other equipment capable of detecting the sex of a foetus to any clinic or person not registered under the Act;
- It prohibits any procedure, technique, test or the administration of anything for the purpose of ensuring or increasing the probability that an embryo will be of a particular sex;
- It requires persons carrying out tests allowed by the Act to keep records;
- It provides for imprisonment of up to five years and a fine of up to Rs. 1,00,000 for violators of the Act;
- It creates state boards to monitor the implementation of the Act and;
- It enlarges the powers of officials to enforce the provisions of the Act.

LEGAL PROVISIONS

Until 1970, the provisions contained in the Indian Penal Code (IPC) governed the law on abortion. The Indian Penal Code 1860 permitted 'legal abortions' done without criminal intent and in good faith for the express purpose of saving the life of the mother. Liberalisation of abortion laws was also advocated as one of the measures of population control. With these considerations, the Medical Termination of Pregnancy Act was passed in July 1971, which came into force in April 1972. This law was conceived as a tool to let the pregnant women decide on the number and frequency of children. It further gave them the right to decide on having or not having the child. However, this good intentioned step was being used to force women to abort the female child. In order to do away with lacunae inherent in previous legislation, the Pre-natal Diagnostic Techniques (Regulation and Prevention of Misuse) Act had to be passed in 1994, which came into force in January 1996. The Act prohibited determination of sex of the foetus and stated punishment for the violation of the provisions. It also provided for mandatory registration of genetic counseling centres, clinics, hospitals, nursing homes, etc. Thus both these laws were meant to protect the childbearing function of the woman and legitimise the purpose for which pre-natal tests and abortions could be carried out. However, in practice we find that these provisions have been misused and are proving against the interest of the females.

The Indian government has conceded that abortion may be carried out if there is –

- Danger to the life of the mother if the pregnancy continues till the child birth,
- Danger to the child by or at risk of being born handicapped, or
- If the woman has conceived the child as a result of rape.

Women are also allowed the right to abortion if they wish to do so in the interest of keeping the family small. However, abortion has to be done within a specific period when it is difficult to identify the sex of the foetus. If the abortion is to be carried out after 16-18 weeks of pregnancy, because of any medical reasons, the opinion of two doctors is a must. Unlike abortion, female foeticide is usually done beyond the legal period i.e. when the foetus is much older and developed, and is done only because the foetus is a girl.

Female foeticide is a punishable offence in India. The offenders (both doctor and parents) may be imprisoned or fined or both. The first is the right to life of the unborn child. The second right violated is that of the woman's right over her body. Often the decision not to have the child is taken by the man (husband) or the family and the opinion of the mother who painfully bears the child is rarely considered. At the macro level, this has an impact on the sex ratio of the country.

The main law for prosecuting persons who are engaging in sex selective abortion is the Pre-Natal Diagnostic Techniques (Regulation and Prevention of Misuse) Act, 1994. The PNDT Act now stands renamed as the Pre-Conception and Pre-Natal Diagnostic Techniques Act, 2003.

Techniques from (Prohibition of Sex selection) Act from 2003;

- It prohibits misuse and advertisement of pre-natal diagnostic techniques for determination of sex of foetus, leading to female foeticide.
- It permits and regulates the use of pre-natal diagnostic techniques for detection of specific genetic abnormalities or disorders and use of such techniques only under certain conditions and only by the registered institutions.
- It provides for punishment for violation of the provisions given in the act.
- The complaint made by any person should be first given to the appropriate authority with the notice of not less than thirty days for proper action and with the intention to make a complaint to the court.

Apart from this law, the following sections from the Indian Penal Code, 1860 are also important –

Section-299 Culpable Homicide

"Whoever causes death by doing an act with the intention of causing death, or with the intention of causing such bodily injury as is likely to cause death, or with the knowledge that he is likely by such act to cause death commits the offence of culphable homicide."

Explanation 3 state that the causing of the death of a child in the mother's womb is not homicide. But it may amount to culpable homicide to cause the death of a living child if any part of that child has been brought forth, though the child may not have breathed or been completely born.

Comment: This explanation does not treat death of a child in the mother's womb. A homicide but if any part of a living child is brought forth causing its death may amount to culpable homicide even though the child may not have breathing or it may not have been completely born. In other words, killing of a pregnant woman is only one homicide and not homicides because as long as a child is in the mother's womb it has no independent existence of its own. But if any part of a child has come out of its mother's womb and the child is a living child, causing its death may amount to culpable homicide if requirements mentioned in any of the clauses of section 299 are fulfilled. For this it is not necessary that the child must have breathed or it may have been completely born, it is important to note, however, that an act done with intent to prevent a child from being born alive or to cause it to die after its birth is a punishable offence under section 315 of Code.

Section 312: Causing miscarriage

"Whoever voluntarily causes a woman with child to miscarry, shall, if such miscarriage be not caused in good faith for the purpose of saving the life of the woman, be punished with imprisonment of either description for a term which may extend to three years, or with fine, or with both; and, if the woman be quick with child, shall be punished with imprisonment of either description for a term which may extend to seven years, and shall be also liable to fine.

Explanation – A woman who causes herself to miscarry, is within the meaning of this section."

In Queen Emp. v. Aruna Bewa[2] where pregnancy was almost mature and an attempt a miscarriage resulted in the birth of child, it was held that a conviction under section 312 was bad in law but the accused guilty under section 312 read with section 511 for attempting to cause miscarriage.

A case of female foeticide, T.K. Rajalakshmi[3] from Fatehgarh Sahib district in Punjab and a two-day consultation on foeticide in the State underline the need to tackle the menace in full swing.

There is a mood of disquiet in Kale Majra village in Punjab's Fatehgarh Sahib district. A little over 50 km from Chandigarh which represents a modern city of the 21st century, Fatehgarh Sahib has the dubious distinction of being the district with the lowest juvenile sex ratio in the country. The mood is even more gloomy today in the house of Gurmeet Singh and his brothers. In March, Gurmeet Singh's wife Surinder Kaur and his sister-in-law Devender Kaur were arrested by the police on charges of aborting a female foetus. They were both charged under Section 312 and 120 of the Indian Penal Code, 1860. The provisions of the Pre-Natal Diagnostic Techniques (Regulation and Prevention of Misuse) Act, 1994 have not been invoked. A staff nurse who allegedly performed the abortion was booked under the Medical Termination of Pregnancy (MTP) Act, T.K. Rajalakshmi, Surinder Kaur, who stands accused of foeticide, at home in Kale Majra village of Fatehgarh district, with her three-year-old daughter and husband Gurmeet Singh.

No action has been taken against a diagnostic centre that is allegedly involved. The sections that can be invoked here include Section 5(2) which prohibits any person conducting pre-natal diagnostic procedures from communicating to the pregnant woman or her relative, the sex of the foetus by means of words, signs or in any other manner; Section 6(b) which prohibits the determination of the sex of the foetus and Section 20(3) which empowers the Appropriate Authority (in this case, the Chief Medical Officer of Fatehgarh Sahib district) to suspend in public interest the registration of the clinic or laboratory without issuing any show-cause notice. This power has not been invoked as yet by the Appropriate Authority and according to Veena Kumari, coordinator of Human Rights Law Network, the woman doctor who was running the diagnostic centre had shifted her operations elsewhere. The ultrasonologist involved was not to be found either. Two women in Bhatinda district have also been similarly booked under Section 312 IPC.

The MTP Act, 1971 legalises abortion though it lays down several conditions under which such a procedure may be performed. Section 120 pertains to concealing a design to commit an offence and this is punishable with imprisonment.

In the year 1971 the Parliament enacted the Medical Termination of Pregnancy Act 1971 with a view to liberalise abortions and also minimize illegal abortions which have been taking place in India on a large scale, mostly by quacks. The Act, a small one with only eight sections, recognises a woman's right to privacy, space and limit pregnancy and take decisions with respect to her own body. Encouragement to bring down population growth rate and permitting terminating unwanted pregnancy of a married woman, because of failure of contraceptive device, are other important features of the Act. The pregnancy can be terminated only by a registered medical practitioner where there is a risk of life of a pregnant woman, or risk of grave injury to her physical or mental health or the pregnancy is caused by rape, or a substantial risk exists to the effect that if the child is born it would be severely handicapped because of physical or mental abnormalities, or where contraceptive method of a married woman has failed, or exists a risk to her health because of her actual or reasonably foreseeable environment.

The offence under this section is non-cognizable, bailable and non-compoundable and is triable by magistrate of the first class where miscarriage falls under the first part of the section, and by court of session where it falls under the latter part it.

Section 315: Act done with intent to prevent child being born alive or to cause it to die after birth–

Whoever before the birth of any child does any act with the intention of thereby preventing that child from being born alive or causing it to die after its birth, and does by such act prevent that child from being born alive, or causes it to die after its birth, shall, if such act be not caused in good faith for the purpose of saving the life of the mother, be punished with imprisonment of either description for a term which may extend to ten years, or with fine, or with both.

The duty to prove a case is on the prosecution and if it fails in its duty, an accused could not be held guilty on basis of mere suspicion Leelawati vs. State.[4]

The offence under this section is cognizable, non-bailable and non-compoundable, triable by court of session.

Section 316: Causing death of quick unborn child by act amounting to culpable homicide–

"Whoever does any act under such circumstances, that if thereby caused death he would be guilty of culpable homicide; and does such act cause the death of a quick unborn child, shall be punished with the imprisonment of either description for a term which may extend to ten years, and shall also be liable to fine."

Where the accused husband struck his wife who was twenty weeks pregnant as a result of which both his wife and child were killed, it was held that the accused was guilty under this section in addition to his guilt under section 302 of the Code.[5]

The offence under section 316 is cognizable, non-bailable and non-compoundable, and is triable by court of session.

Section 317: Exposure and abandonment of child under twelve years by parent or person having care of it–

"Whoever being the father or mother of a child under the age of twelve years, or having the care of such child, shall expose or leave such child in any place with the intention of wholly abandoning such child, shall be punished with imprisonment of either description for a term which may extend to seven years, or with fine, or with both."

Section 318. Concealment of birth by secret disposal of dead body–

"Whoever, secretly burying or otherwise disposing of the dead body of a child whether such child dies before or after or during its birth, intentionally conceals or endeavours to conceal the birth of such child, shall be punished with imprisonment of either description for a term which may extend to two years, or with fine, or with both."

Where the accused gave birth to a child in a village jungle and soon after the birth it died and the, accused left it there, this could not be held to be a secret disposal under this section.[6]

Delivering a dead child in the compound of her house by the accused mother and then leaving it there and telling no one about it is not an offence under this section.[7]

The punishment for these offences extends from two years up to life imprisonment, or fine or both.

NOTES

1. 2001 (5) SCC 577: AIR 2001 SC 2007
2. (1873)19 WR CD 32.
3. T.K. Rajalakshmi in Chandigarh and Fatehgarh Sahib, Vol. 19 - Issue 12, June 8, 21, 2002.
4. Leelawati v. State. 1982 Cr LJ 27 (P & H).
5. Murugan v. State, 1991 Cr LJ 1680 (Mad).
6. Saraswati Vs Emp. (1905) 2 Cr.L.J. 667.
7. Amina v. Emp., (1892) Cr C. 607.

5

Suggestion and Conclusion

Modify the MTP Act

Bring an amendment in the Medical Termination of Pregnancy Act of 1971. Pregnancy termination should not be allowed after 12 weeks. Under the present Act, it is allowed up to 20 weeks of gestation. Pregnancy termination after 12 weeks should be allowed only if the life of the mother is in danger or the foetus has congenital malformations. Septic abortion is still a major cause of maternal mortality even after liberalisation of abortion. Allowing it in private nursing homes will result in an increase in female foeticide, as it is now. Though the government has taken steps to ban the ultrasound laboratories for diagnosis of antenatal sex, it is not going to help since most such centres do not give the authorisation in writing. Second trimester termination of pregnancy is still being carried out mostly in private sector. Over 90 per cent of terminations for limitation of family size are done before 12 weeks and the safest period is 6-8 weeks of gestation and diagnosis can be made by use of ultrasound and pregnancy kits. Barring a few countries, the abortion law is liberalised, and in many of those countries it is allowed only up to 12 weeks. Most of pregnancy terminations (10 per cent in second trimester) are for female foeticide.

Educate Women

Some of the basic causes for female foeticide are dowry, pre-diagnostic techniques and the belief that only a son can look after his parents. Social awareness and women's education are what we need to combat this situation. If women are aware of their rights and get better job opportunities, social outlook towards the girl child will change. Religious institution can do a lot in bringing about a social change. Besides, pre-diagnostic law should be stern.

Social Awakening is Needed

Spread the awareness in society that female foeticide is a sin and religion also needs to allow women to have equal rights as men. We need to preach that an imbalance in sex ratio will create a severe shortage of brides in future. If dowry system ends, more and more couples would want to bring girl child into this world. All doctors who aid female foeticide should lose their licences and death should be the only penalty for them.

Ease Burden on Girl's Family

The government should take steps to provide girls with free education, interest-free loans (to be self-reliant) and reservation in jobs and educational institutes, so that everyone thinks it's not a shame to bear a girl child. We can't continue to live as murderers of unborn girls.

Make This Offence Non-Bailable

Female foeticide is now carried out in total secrecy, otherwise there's no reason that the sex ratio should not improve. A strict implementation of the PCPNDT Act is needed. Doctors should lose their licences, if found aiding this practice. Officials monitoring the implementation of the PCPNDT Act should be more efficient. Any woman undergoing sex-determination test should be booked and her husband should automatically be made co-accused. Female foeticide should be a non-bailable offence. A foolproof intelligence network needs to be built up to detect cases of female foeticide.

An atmosphere of fear needs to be created for anybody indulging in female foeticide.

Status of Women

The best way to stop female foeticide is to raise the status of women to such an extent that couples start having female babies as a matter of choice. Laws, however stringent, can't control such problems. The concept of daughters as "*Paraya Dhan*" should change to "*Apna Dhan*". All reservation for women should be abolished, as the word reservation is linked with backwardness. Media should not sensationalise any news related with women. Education for all should be made compulsory.

Make Medical Councils Step In

The government, NGOs, women and child-development organisations should join hands to create awareness among the masses about the ill effects of female foeticide. No Act alone can eradicate the menace. The medical councils should issue directives to all doctors that they should either desist from conducting foetal sex determination and committing female foeticide or be held guilty of professional misconduct. Women empowerment and girl-child education is of paramount importance because literacy leads to confidence, independence, awareness, self-respect and sensibility.

Force Doctor to Record Abortions

Nearly one million girls are being killed in the womb in India each year. Doctors aiding this mass murder make Rs. 500 crore or so each year, mainly due to our prejudice against the girl child. It is a sign of our backwardness that the birth of a male child is welcome, whereas, the birth of a female child is an occasion for mourning. Techniques like ultrasound sonography have made it possible for us to know the sex of an unborn child. The inventors of the machine might not have imagined that it would become an instrument of mass murder. Raid the nursing homes and clinics and force the doctors there to keep a record of all abortions. Punish the guilty and cancel their licences; if need be, even prosecute these persons.

Desperate Remedy is Needed

Apart from creating social awakening, we should take strict action against clinics and nursing homes promoting pre-natal sex determination. Special cells should be formed for monitoring these houses of murder. All clinics found carrying out pre-natal sex-determination and female foeticide should be closed straightaway. Desperate situations demand desperate remedy.

Conclusion and Policy Suggestions

It can be concluded from the present study that majority of the respondents approved of female foeticide under one pretext or the other. Dowry was cited as the main reason behind it. Daughters were unable to provide social security to their parents in old age and thus were considered an unnecessary investment. At the same time, respondents were apprehensive of finding a suitable match for their male children. The following suggestive measures flew out from the study:

1. Laws have been passed declaring female foeticide as illegal. Advertising for prenatal prediction of sex has also been declared illegal. Efforts should be made to implement these laws effectively. Strict punishment should be given to the defaulters.
2. The trend of taking and giving of dowry which takes place mostly in educated and upper class homes can not be discouraged by laws alone. It is entrenched in the mindset of India's people and no amount of preaching would stop it. However efforts should continue to be made at the individual as well as at the government level. Stringent and effective laws should be supported by speedy trials, dowry giving and taking cases should be tried by a special court and short stay homes should be set up for battered women.
3. Efforts and provisions should be made to provide social security to parents who are above 65 years of age and have only daughters. They should be provided with old age pension if they do not have a son. Most of the respondents in the study who had daughters feared for their social security especially in old age.
4. Girl children should be provided free and compulsory education up to higher secondary level. This would decrease the so-called

"unnecessary investment on girl children" made by the parents on their daughters. They would stop taking their daughters as a liability, which many respondents taken for the study did grumble about.

5. Certain schemes should be started for providing economic provisions for the female children. For this purpose, government should start various employment schemes for females where 100% reservation could be made for women in occupations like teaching, nursing, as telephone operators etc.
6. Women's right to own and inherit property and the social obligation of daughters to support parents in the same way as sons, can be spread by policy intervention to inculcate these new values in households as well as legal support to implement these values should be provided.
7. The Ministry of Women and Child Welfare should dispatch congratulatory greetings to couples who attain parenthood with the birth of a girl child. Many respondents in the study felt shame and embarrassment about having many daughters. The government by dispatching such greetings could spread awareness that the birth of a girl is a joyous occasion and would instill confidence in the mother who usually finds herself at the receiving end whenever a girl child is born.
8. Religious education can play a role by preaching against female foeticide, dowry and discrimination against the girl children.
9. Moral education should be imparted in schools. Children should be taught to uphold morals and refrain from practices of dowry, female foeticide, gender bias. The vulnerable minds of the children should be so influenced that they grow up as adults who consider practicing dowry and female foeticide as immoral.
10. Various monetary benefits should be provided to parents having daughters.
11. Women should also be socialized from early childhood to consider themselves as equal to men. They should be encouraged to assume all those responsibilities, which are normally considered to be belonging to the male domain. This would be a positive influence on the coming generations as today's girl child would be tomorrow's mother as well as mother-in-law.
12. Analysis at the city and town level could help to identify gender

discrimination trends which could help the government and non- government organisations combat female foeticide and infanticide.

13. Governments and organisations could also learn from cities which have a healthy gender ratio: Puducherry, Aizawl (Mizoram), Kolar (Karnataka), Kumbkonam (Tamil Nadu) and Nagercoil (Tamil Nadhu).
14. The suggestive measures which flew unabated from the study included strict implementation of laws banning female foeticide and dowry, providing old age pension for parents who had no son, free and compulsory education for girls, job reservation for women in specific occupations and giving them an equal share in the property, in the true sense of the word.

Female Foeticide in India is a genocide of one million women annually with tragic consequences. Urgent steps need to be taken to immediately end this genocide and prevent its tragic consequences. This could lead to 10 per cent of men being unmarried, leading to immense increase in rapes, HIV/AIDS, criminal activity, depression and suicide. The easiest way to end this genocide is to ban private ultrasound clinics. Till such legislation is enacted, the PCPNDT cell must be strengthened with staff strength of 1000 officers to monitor 30,000 ultrasound clinics. It is also important for government to amend the Dowry Prohibition Act so that a cap is put on marriage expenses at 20 per cent of annual income of father. A cell with 10,000 officers should be created to implement the dowry prohibition act.

There are two approaches to the demographic imbalance. The first, considered as utilitarian, concerns mainly the potential scarcity of women in the years to come, and there will be fewer women to fulfil certain key social roles including reproduction, child care, marriage and domestic work. The documentary film 'Daughters of Gardener (Marceau, 2007)[1], shows that already a lot of young men cannot find wives. A second approach, more critical, produces a reflection on the structural aspects of the problem by questioning power relations, gender stereotypes and patriarchal values of the India society. Indeed, the demographic imbalance worries researchers and politicians because social implications are still uncertain but could lead to, for example, an increase in wives trafficking, gang rape and polyandrous marriages.[2] Some films are dealing with the subject including *Matrabhoomi: A Nation without Women*.[3]

Currently some factors keep or even accentuate demographic imbalance and sex-selective abortion: a powerful medical lobby which does not wish to eradicate these paid services; a lack of political will; an inability to implement the law and to control 'doctors and technicians' practices. The solutions around this phenomenon are not obvious, even if the Indian Media have been warning about the lack of women for over 15 years.

Seeing itself as the largest democracy in the world, the Indian State was provided a broad legislative and legal device that wishes to defend the rights of its citizen, including women. Moreover, equality between men and women is in the Indian Constitution. To counter the dispossession of women, a law was amended, giving women the right to inherit and become joint owner of the common goods as well as their brothers. In addition, they can become sole owners and managers of the land inherited. In 2005, the Indian state created a decree requiring all marriages to be civilly registered, to counter precariat in case of rejection from the husband. Women can also reside in the home of their parents after their wedding, which was prohibited before. A decree on the protection of women against domestic violence was voted in 2006 to provide more legal power to women in family affairs. India's federal government seeks to include women's rights into its policies and improve their living conditions.

The average sex ratio in the largest 500 Indian cities - the total population (221 million) of which is nearly equal to that of the United Kingdom, France, Germany & Spain combined - was 902. Sex-ratio in Indian cities as bad or worse than those found in rural India in 2011, which has about 923 females per 1000 males.

India's sex-ratio at birth - the number of girls born for every

1000 boys - since 2011 has slightly improved, from 902 girls per 1000 boys in 2011 to 903 girls in 2015, according to data from the World Bank.

But this ratio is still the fifth worst in the world, better than only Liechtenstein (794), China (867), Azerbaizan (879) and Armenia (883). India's sex-ratio is worse than Pakistan (920), South Korea (952), Nigeria (944) and Nepal (939) according to World Bank.

As per Statistical Report-2015, sex-ratio at birth is 900 females per 1000 males. It has gone down from 906 in 2011 in Urban areas it is 890. The worse state Haryana 831 females/1000 males. It has gone down from 854 in 2011. In urban Haryana it is 821 females/1000 males. The situation is worse in urban areas of almost all states.

Government may preach *Beti Bachao* but sex-ratio is still skewed in big cities and only getting worse.

An adverse child sex-ratio is also reflected in the distorted gender makeup of the entire population. In 2031 India will have

936 females per 1000 males, which will be lower than its 1951 sex ratio of 946 females per 1000 males (as world bank predicted).

"*Yatra Naranthya Pujyathe Raman the Tatra Devatha*" has been India's culture. In India a girl is worshiped as a Devi on one hand and denied her existence on the other as if she has no right to live. Time has perhaps come for us to get rid of male chauvinism and treat children as gifts of nature regardless of their gender. We cannot imagine a society in the future where there will be only males and no females. The society will be full of crimes and evils. Only if legislations enacted in this behalf are not sufficient. Orthodox views regarding women need to be changed. The PCPNDT Act should penalize and punish the violators of this crime strictly. The pernicious acts of female foeticide and coercive abortions have to end before women becomes endangered species.

NOTES

1. Daughters of Gardeners (2007) Directed by Karina Marceau Montreal : Cinefete.
2. Croll e (2000) Endangered Daughters, London, Routledge.
3. Matrubhoomi : A Nationa without women (2005) directed by Manish Jha, Patrick Sobelman, Punkej Kharbanda Production.

Annexures

ANNEXURE – I

THE PRE-CONCEPTION AND PRE-NATAL DIAGNOSTIC TECHNIQUES (PROHIBITION OF SEX SELECTION) ACT, 1994

(Act No. 57 of 1994) [20th September, 1994]

An Act to provide for the prohibition of sex selection, before or after conception, and for regulation of pre-natal diagnostic techniques for the purposes of detecting genetic abnormalities or metabolic disorders or chromosomal abnormalities or certain congenital malformations or sex-linked disorders and for the prevention of their misuse for sex determination leading to female foetcide; and for matters connected therewith or incidental thereto.[1]

Be, it enacted by Parliament in the Forty-fifth Year of the Republic of India as follows:

(I) PRELIMINARY

1. Short title, extent and commencement –

(1) This Act may be called [the Pre-conception and Pre-natal Diagnostic Techniques (Prohibition of Sex Selection)] Act, 1994.[2]

(2) It shall extend to the whole of India except the State of Jammu and Kashmir.

(3) It shall come into force on such date[3] as the Central Government may, by notification in the Official Gazette, appoint.

2. Definitions – In this Act, unless the context otherwise requires,

(a) "Appropriate Authority" means the Appropriate Authority appointed under section 17;

(b) "Board" means the Central Supervisory Board constituted under section 7;

[4](ba) "conceptus" means any product of conception at any stage of development from fertilisation until birth including extra embryonic membranes as well as the embryo or foetus;

(bb) "embryo" means a developing human organism after fertilisation till the end of eight weeks (fifty-six days);

(bc) "foetus" means a human organism during the period of its development beginning on the fifty-seventh day following fertilisation or creation (excluding any time in which its development has been suspended) and ending at the birth;

(c) "Genetic Counseling Centre" means an institute, hospital, nursing home or any place, by whatever name called, which provides for genetic counseling to patients;

(d) "Genetic Clinic" means a clinic, institute, hospital, nursing home or any place, by whatever name called, which is used for conducting pre-natal diagnostic procedures.

[5]**Explanation**– For the purposes of this clause, "Genetic Clinic' includes a vehicle, where ultrasound machine or imaging machine or scanner or other equipment capable of determining sex of the foetus or a portable equipment which has the potential for detection of sex during pregnancy or selection of sex before conception, is used.

(e) "Genetic Laboratory" means a laboratory and includes a place where facilities are provided for conducting analysis or tests of samples received from Genetic Clinic for pre-natal diagnostic test.

Explanation– For the purposes of this clause, "Genetic Laboratory' includes a place where ultrasound machine or imaging machine or scanner or other equipment capable of determining sex of the foetus or a portable equipment which has the potential for detection of sex during pregnancy or selection of sex before conception, is used.

(f) "Gynaecologist" means a person who possesses a post-graduate qualification in gynaecology and obstetrics;

[6](g) "Medical Geneticist" includes a person who possesses a degree or diploma in genetic science in the fields of sex selection and pre-natal diagnostic techniques or has experience of not less than two years in such field after obtaining–

(i) any one of the medical qualifications recognised under the Indian Medical Council Act, 1956 (102 of 1956); or

(ii) a post-graduate degree in biological sciences;

(h) "Pediatrician" means a person who possesses a post-graduate qualification in paediatrics;

[7](i) "pre-natal diagnostic procedures" means all gynaecological or obstetrical or medical procedures such as ultrasonography, foetoscopy, taking or removing samples of amniotic fluid, chorionic villi, blood or any other tissue or fluid of a man, or of a woman, for being sent to a Genetic Laboratory or Genetic Clinic for conducting any type of analysis or pre-natal diagnostic tests for selection of sex before or after conception;

(j) "pre-natal diagnostic techniques" includes all pre-natal diagnostic procedures and pre-natal diagnostic tests;

[8](k) "pre-natal diagnostic test" means ultrasonography or any test or analysis of amniotici fluid, chorionic villi, blood or any tissue or fluid of a pregnant woman or conceptus conducted to detect genetic or metabolic disorders or chromosomal abnormalities or congenital anomalies or haemoglobinopathies or sex-linked diseases;

(l) "prescribed" means prescribed by rules made under this Act;

(m) "registered medical practitioner" means a medical practitioner who possesses any recognised medical qualification as defined in clause (h) of section 2 of the Indian Medical Council Act, 1956 (102 of 1956), and whose name has been entered in a State Medical Register;

(n) "regulations" means regulations framed by the Board under this Act;

[9](o) "sex selection" includes any procedure, technique, test or administration or prescription or provision of anything for the purpose of ensuring or increasing the probability that an embryo will be of a particular sex;

(p) "sonologist or imaging specialist" means a person who possesses any one of the medical qualifications recognised under the Indian Medical Council Act, 1956 (102 of 1956) or who possesses a post-graduate qualification in ultrasonography or imaging techniques or radiology;

(q) "State Board" means a State Supervisory Board or a Union territory Supervisory Board constituted under section 16A;

(r) "State Government" in relation to Union territory with Legislature means the Administrator of that Union territory appointed by the President under article 239 of Constitution.

(II) REGULATION OF GENETIC COUNSELING CENTRES, GENETIC LABORATORIES AND GENETIC CLINICS

3. Regulation of Genetic Counseling Centres, Genetic Laboratories and Genetic Clinics– On and from the commencement of this Act, –

(1) no Genetic Counseling Centre, Genetic Laboratory or Genetic Clinic unless registered under this Act, shall conduct or associate with, or help in, conducting activities relating to pre-natal diagnostic techniques;

[10](2) no Genetic Counseling Centre or Genetic Laboratory or Genetic Clinic shall employ or cause to be employed or take services of any person, whether on honorary basis or on payment who does not possess qualifications as may be prescribed;

(3) no medical geneticist, gynaecologist, paediatrician, registered medical practitioner or any other person shall conduct or cause to be conducted or aid in conducting by himself or through any other person, any pre-natal diagnostic techniques at a place other than a place registered under this Act.

Comments– Genetic Counseling Centers, Genetics Laboratories, Genetic Clinics, unless registered under the Act, can conduct or associate with, or help in, conducting activities relating to pre-natal diagnostic techniques. They cannot employ or cause to be employed or take services of any person whether on honorary basis or on payment who does not possess the pre-scribed qualifications. Medical geneticist, gynaecologist, pediatrician, registered medical practitioner or any other person cannot conduct or cause to be conduced or aid in conducting by himself or through any other person, any pre-natal diagnostic techniques at a place other than a registered place.

[11](3A) Prohibition of sex-selection – No person, including a specialist or a team of specialists in the field of infertility, shall conduct or cause to be conducted or aid in conducting by himself or by any other person, sex selection on a woman or a man or on both or on any tissue, embryo, conceptus, fluid or gametes derived from either or both of them.

Comments– Sex selection on a woman or a man or on both or on any tissue, embryo, conceptus, fluid or gametes derived from either or both of them is prohibited.

(3B) Prohibition on sale of ultrasound machine, etc., to persons, laboratories, clinics, etc., not registered under the Act. – No person shall sell any ultrasound machine or imaging machine or scanner or any other equipment capable of detecting sex of foetus to any Genetic Counseling Centre, Genetic Laboratory, Genetic Clinic or any other person not registered under the Act.

Comments– Sale of any ultrasound machine or imaging machine or scanner or any other equipment capable of detecting sex of foetus to any Genetic Counseling Center, Genetic Laboratory, Genetic Clinic or any other person not registered under the Act is prohibited.

(III) REGULATION OF PRE-NATAL DIAGNOSTIC TECHNIQUES

4. Regulation of pre-natal diagnostic techniques– on and from the commencement of this Act, –

(1) no place including a registered Genetic Counseling Centre or Genetic Laboratory or Genetic Clinic shall be used or caused to be used by any person for conducting pre-natal diagnostic techniques except for the purposes specified in clause (2) and after satisfying any of the conditions specified in clause (3);

(2) no pre-natal diagnostic techniques shall be conducted except for the purposes of detection of any of the following abnormalities, namely:

- (i) chromosomal abnormalities;
- (ii) genetic metabolic diseases;
- (iii) haemoglobinopathies;
- (iv) sex-linked genetic diseases;

(v) congenital anomalies;

(vi) any other abnormalities or diseases as may be specified by the Central Supervisory Board[12];

[13](3) no pre-natal diagnostic techniques shall be used or conducted unless the person qualified to do so is satisfied for reasons to be recorded in writing that any of the following conditions are fulfilled, namely:

(i) age of the pregnant woman is above thirty-five years;

(ii) the pregnant woman has undergone two or more spontaneous abortions or foetal loss;

(iii) the pregnant woman had been exposed to potentially teratogenic agents such as drugs, radiation, infection or chemicals;

(iv) the pregnant woman or her spouse has a family history of mental retardation or physical deformities such as, spasticity or any other genetic disease;

(v) any other condition as may be specified by the Central Supervisory Board:

Provided that the person conducting ultrasonography on a pregnant woman shall keep complete record thereof in the clinic in such manner, as may be prescribed, and any deficiency or inaccuracy found therein shall amount to contravention of the provisions of section 5 or section 6 unless contrary is proved by the person conducting such ultrasonography;

(4) no person including a relative or husband of the pregnant woman shall seek or encourage the conduct of any pre-natal diagnostic techniques on her except for the purposes specified in clause (2);

(5) no person including a relative or husband of a woman shall seek or encourage the conduct of any sex-selection technique on her or him or both.

5. Written consent of pregnant woman and prohibition of communicating the sex of foetus–

(1) No person referred to in clause (2) of section 3 shall conduct the pre-natal diagnostic procedures unless–

(a) he has explained all known side and after effects of such procedures to the pregnant woman concerned;

(b) he has obtained in the prescribed form her written consent to undergo such procedures in the language which she understands; and;

(c) a copy of her written consent obtained under clause (b) is given to the pregnant woman.

[14](2) No person including the person conducting pre-natal diagnostic procedures shall communicate to the pregnant woman concerned or her relatives or any other person the sex of the foetus by words, signs, or in any other manner.

Comments– Pre-natal diagnostic procedures cannot be conducted unless (i) all side and after effects of such procedures have been explained to the concerned pregnant woman, (ii) her written consent to undergo such procedures has been obtained in the language which she understands, and (iii) a copy of her written consent is given to the concerned pregnant woman. Communication of sex of the foetus by words, signs or in any other manner to the concerned pregnant woman or her relatives or any other person is prohibited.

6. Determination of sex prohibited – On and from the commencement of this Act, –

(a) no Genetic Counseling Centre or Genetic Laboratory or Genetic Clinic shall conduct or cause to be conducted in its Centre, Laboratory or Clinic, pre-natal diagnostic techniques including ultrasonography, for the purpose of determining the sex of a foetus;

(b) no person shall conduct or cause to be conducted any pre-natal diagnostic techniques including ultrasonography for the purpose of determining the sex of a foetus.

[15](c) no person shall, by whatever means, cause or allow to be caused selection of sex before or after conception.

Comments–No Genetic Counseling Centres or Genetic Laboratories or Genetic Clinic or any person can conduct or cause to be conducted pre-natal diagnostic techniques including ultrasonography for the purpose of determining the sex of a foetus. No person can cause or allow to be, caused selection of sex before or after conception.

(IV) CENTRAL SUPERVISORY BOARD

7. Constitution of Central Supervisory Board –

(1) The Central Government shall constitute a Board to be known as the Central Supervisory Board to exercise the powers and perform the functions conferred on the Board under this Act.

(2) The Board shall consist of–

(a) the Minister in charge of the Ministry or Department of Family Welfare, who shall be the Chairman, *ex officio*;

(b) the Secretary to the Government of India in charge of the Department of Family Welfare, who shall be the Vice-Chairman, *ex officio*;

[16](c) three members to be appointed by the Central Government to represent the Ministries of Central Government in charge of Women and Child Development, Department of Legal Affairs or Legislative Department in the Ministry of Law and Justice, and Indian System of Medicine and Homoeopathy, ex officio;

(d) the Director General of Health Services of the Central Government, *ex-officio*;

(e) ten members to be appointed by the Central Government, two each from amongst–

(i) eminent medical geneticists;

[17](ii) eminent gynaecologist and obstetrician or expert *of stri-roga or prasuti-tantra.;*

(iii) eminent paediatricians;

(iv) eminent social scientists; and

(v) representatives of women welfare organisations;

(f) three women Members of Parliament, of whom two shall be elected by the House of the People and one by the Council of States;

(g) four members to be appointed by the Central Government by rotation to represent the States and the Union territories, two in the alphabetical order and two in the reverse alphabetical order:

Provided that no appointment under this clause shall be made except on the recommendation of the State Government or, as the case may be, the Union territory;

(h) an officer, not below the rank of a Joint Secretary or equivalent of the Central Government, in charge of Family Welfare, who shall be the Member-Secretary, *ex officio*.

8. Term of office members –

(1) The term of office of a member, other than an *ex officio* member, shall be:

(a) in case of appointment under clause (e) or clause (f) of sub-section 2) of section 7, three years; [18]

[19]Provided that the term of office of a member elected under clause (f) of sub-section (2) of section 7 shall come to an end as soon as the member becomes a Minister or Minister of State or Deputy Minister, or the Speaker or the Deputy Speaker of the House of the People, or the Deputy Chairman of the Council of States or ceases to be a member of the House from which he was elected; and;

(b) in case of appointment under clause (g) of the said sub-section, one year.

(2) If a casual vacancy occurs in the office of any other members, whether by reason of his death, resignation or inability to discharge his functions owing to illness or other incapacity, such vacancy shall be filled by the Central Government by making a fresh appointment and the member so appointed shall hold office for the remainder of the term of office of the person in whose place he is so appointed.

(3) The Vice-Chairman shall perform such functions as may be assigned to him by the Chairman from time to time.

(4) The procedure to be followed by the members in the discharge of their functions shall be such as may be presented.

9. Meetings of the Board –

(1) The Board shall meet at such time and place, and shall observe such rules of procedure in regard to the transaction of business at its meetings (including the quorum at such meetings) as may be provided by regulations:

Provided that the Board shall meet at least once in six months.

(2) The Chairman and in his absence the Vice-Chairman shall preside at the meetings of the Board.

(3) If for any reason the Chairman or the Vice-Chairman is unable to attend any meeting of the Board, any other member chosen by the members present at the meeting shall preside at the meeting.

(4) All questions which come up before any meeting of the Board shall be decided by a majority of the votes of the members present and voting, and in the event of an equality of votes, the Chairman, or in his absence, the person presiding, shall have and exercise a second or casting vote.

(5) Members other than ex officio members shall receive such allowances, if any, from the Board as may be prescribed.

10. Vacancies, etc., not to invalidate proceedings of the Board– No act or proceeding of the Board shall be invalid merely by reason of–

(a) any vacancy in, or any defect in the constitution of, the Board; or

(b) any defect in the appointment of a person acting as a member of the Board; or

(c) any irregularity in the procedure of the Board not affecting the merits of the case.

11. Temporary association of persons with the Board for particular purposes–

(1) The Board may associate with itself, in such manner and for purposes as may be determined by regulations, any person whose assistance or advice it may desire in carrying out any of the provisions of this Act.

(2) A person associated with it by the Board under sub-section (1) for any purpose shall have a right to take part in the discussions relevant to that purpose, but shall not have a right to vote at a meeting of the Board and shall not be a member for any other purpose.

12. Appointment of officers and other employees of the Board–

(1) For the purpose of enabling it efficiently to discharge its functions under this Act, the Beard may, subject to such regulations as may be made in this behalf, appoint (whether on deputation or otherwise) such number of officers and other employees as it may consider necessary:

Provided that the appointment of such category of officers, as may be specified in such regulations, shall be subject to the approval of the Central Government.

(2) Every officer or other employee appointed by the Board shall be subject to such conditions of service and shall be entitled to such remuneration as may be specified in the regulations.

13. Authentication of orders and other instruments of the Board–All orders and decisions of the Board shall be authenticated by the signature of the Chairman or any other member authorised by the Board in this behalf, and all other instruments issued by the Board shall be authenticated by the signature of the Member-Secretary or any other officer of the Board authorised in like manner in this behalf.

14. Disqualifications for appointment as member–A person shall be disqualified for being appointed as a member if, he–

(a) has been convicted and sentenced to imprisonment for an offence which, in the opinion of the Central Government, involves moral turpitude; or

(b) is an undischarged insolvent; or

(c) is of unsound mind and stands so declared by a competent court; or

(d) has been removed or dismissed from the service of the Government or a Corporation owned or controlled by the Government; or

(e) has, in the opinion of the Central Government, such financial or other interest in the Board as is likely to affect prejudicially the discharge by him of his functions as a member; or

[20](f) has, in the opinion of the Central Government, been associated with the use or promotion of pre-natal diagnostic technique for determination of sex or with any sex selection technique.

15. Eligibility of member for re-appointment–Subject to the other terms and conditions of service as may be prescribed, any person ceasing to be a member shall be eligible for re-appointment as such member:

[21]Provided that no member other than an ex officio member shall be appointed for more than two consecutive terms.

[22]16. **Functions of the Board**– The Board shall have the following functions, namely–

(i) to advise the Central Government on policy matters relating to use of pre-natal diagnostic techniques, sex selection techniques and against their misuse;

(ii) to review and monitor implementation of the Act and rules made there under and recommend to the Central Government changes in the said Act and rules;

(iii) to create public awareness against the practice of pre-conception sex selection and pre-natal determination of sex of foetus leading to female foeticide;

(iv) to lay down code of conduct to be observed by persons working at Genetic counseling Centres, Genetic Laboratories and Genetic Clinics;

(v) to oversee the performance of various bodies constituted under the Act and taken appropriate steps to ensure its proper and effective implementation;

(vi) any other functions as may be prescribed under the Act.

[23]16A. **Constitution of State Supervisory Board and Union territory Supervisory Board**–

(1) Each State and Union territory having Legislature shall constitute a Board to be known as the State Supervisory Board or the Union territory Supervisory Board, as the case may be, which shall have the following functions–

(i) to create public awareness against the practice of pre-conception sex selection and pre-natal determination of sex of foetus leading to female foeticide in the State;

(ii) to review the activities of the Appropriate Authorities functioning in the State and recommend appropriate action against them;

(iii) to monitor the implementation of provisions of the Act and the rules and make suitable recommendations relating thereto, to the Board;

(iv) to send such consolidated reports as may be prescribed in respect of various activities undertaken in the State under the Act to the Board and the Central Government; and

(v) any other functions as may be prescribed under the Act.

(2) The State Board shall consist of,

(a) the Minister in charge of Health and Family Welfare in the State, who shall be the Chairperson, ex officio;

(b) the Secretary in charge of the Department of Health and Family Welfare who shall be the Vice-Chairperson, ex officio;

(c) Secretaries or Commissioners in charge of Departments of Women and Child Development, Social Welfare, Law and Indian System of Medicines and Homoeopathy, ex officio, or their representatives;

(d) Director of Health and Family Welfare or Indian System of Medicines and Homoeopathy of the State Government, ex officio;

(e) three women members of Legislative Assembly or Legislative Council;

(f) ten members to be appointed by the State Government out of which two each shall be from the following categories–

(i) eminent social scientists and legal experts;

(ii) eminent women activists from non-governmental organisations or otherwise;

(iii) eminent gynaecologists and obstetricians or experts of *stri-roga* or *prasuti-tantra*;

(iv) eminent paediatricians or medical geneticists;

(v) eminent radiologists or sonologists;

(g) an officer not below the rank of Joint Director in charge of Family Welfare, who shall be the Member Secretary, ex officio.

(3) The State Board shall meet at least once in four months.

(4) The term of office of a member, other than an ex officio member, shall be three years.

(5) If a vacancy occurs in the office of any member other than an ex officio member, it shall be filled by making fresh appointment.

(6) If a member of the Legislative Assembly or member of the Legislative Council who is a member of the State Board,

becomes Minister or Speaker or Deputy Speaker of the Legislative Assembly or Chairperson or Deputy Chairperson of the Legislative Council, he shall cease to be a member of the State Board.

(7) One-third of the total number of members of the State Board shall constitute the Quorum.

(8) The State Board may co-opt a member as and when required, provided that the number of co-opted members does not exceed one-third of the total strength of the State Board.

(9) The co-opted members shall have the same powers and functions as other members, except the right to vote and shall abide by the rules and regulations.

(10) In respect of matters not specified in this section, the State Board shall follow procedures and conditions as are applicable to the Board.

(V) APPROPRIATE AUTHORITY AND ADVISORY COMMITTEE

17. Appropriate Authority and Advisory Committee–

(1) The Central Government shall appoint, by notification in the Official Gazette, one or more Appropriate Authorities for each of the Union territories for the purposes of this Act.

(2) The State Government shall appoint, by notification in the Official Gazette, one or more Appropriate Authorities for the whole or part of the State for the purposes of this Act having regard to the intensity of the problem of pre-natal sex determination leading to female foeticide.

(3) The officers appointed as Appropriate Authorities under sub-section (1) or sub-section (2) shall be,–

[24](a) when appointed for the whole of the State or the Union territory, consisting of the following three members–

(i) an officer of or above the rank of the Joint Director of Health and Family Welfare–Chairperson;

(ii) an eminent woman representing women's organisation; and

(iii) an officer of Law Department of the State or the Union territory concerned:

Provided that it shall be the duty of the State or the Union territory concerned to constitute multi-member State or Union territory level Appropriate Authority within three months of the coming into force of the Pre-natal Diagnostic Techniques (Regulation and Prevention of Misuse) Amendment Act, 2002:

Provided further that any vacancy occurring therein shall be filled within three months of the occurrence;

(b) when appointed for any part of the State or the Union territory, of such other rank as the State Government or the Central Government, as the case may be, may deem fit.

(4) The Appropriate– Authority shall have the following functions namely-

(a) to grant, suspend or cancel registration of a Genetic Counseling Centre, Genetic Laboratory or Genetic Clinic;

(b) to enforce standards prescribed for the Genetic Counseling Centre, Genetic Laboratory and Genetic Clinic;

(c) to investigate complaints of breach of the provisions of this Act or the rules made there under and take immediate action;

(d) to seek and consider the advice of the Advisory Committee, constituted under sub-section (5), on application for registration and on complaints for suspension or cancellation of registration;

[25](e) to take appropriate legal action against the use of any sex selection technique by any person at anyplace, suo motu or brought to its notice and also to initiate independent investigations in such matter;

(f) to create public awareness against the practice of sex selection or pre-natal determination of sex;

(g) to supervise the implementation of the provisions of the Act and rules;

(h) to recommend to the CSB and State Boards modifications required in the rules in accordance with changes in technology or social conditions;

(i) to take action on the recommendations of the Advisory Committee made after investigation of complaint for suspension or cancellation of registration.

(5) The Central Government or the State Government, as the case may be, shall constitute an Advisory Committee for each Appropriate Authority to aid and advise the Appropriate Authority in the discharge of its functions, and shall appoint one of the members of the Advisory Committee to be its Chairman.

(6) The Advisory Committee shall consist of–

(a) three medical experts from amongst gynaecologists, obstericians, paediatricians and medical geneticists;

(b) one legal expert;

(c) one officer to represent the department dealing with information and publicity of the State Government or the Union Territory, as the case may be;

(d) three eminent social workers of whom not less than one shall be from amongst representatives of women's organisations.

[26](7) No person who has been associated with the use or promotion of pre-natal diagnostic techniques for determination of sex or sex selection shall be appointed as a member of the Advisory Committee.

(8) The Advisory Committee may meet as and when it thinks fit or on the request of the Appropriate Authority for consideration of any application for registration or any complaint for suspension or cancellation of registration and to give advice thereon:

Provided that the period intervening between any two meetings shall not exceed the prescribed period.

(9) The terms and conditions subject to which a person may be appointed to the Advisory Committee and the procedure to be followed by such Committee in the discharge of its functions shall be such as may be prescribed.

[27]**17A. Powers of Appropriate Authorities**– The Appropriate Authority shall have the powers in respect of the following matters, namely–

(a) summoning of any person who is in possession of any information relating to violation of the provisions of this Act or the rules made there under;

(b) production of any document or material object relating to clause (a);

(c) issuing search warrant for any place suspected to be indulging in sex selection techniques or pre-natal sex determ nation; and

(d) any other matter which may be prescribed.

(VI) REGISTRATION OF GENETIC COUNSELING CENTRES, GENETIC LABORATORIES AND GENETIC CLINICS

18. Registration of Genetic Counseling Centres, Genetic Laboratories or Genetic Clinics[28]–

(1) No person shall open any Genetic Counseling Centre, Genetic Laboratory or Genetic Clinic, including clinic, laboratory or centre having ultrasound or imaging machine or scanner or any other technology capable of undertaking determination of sex of foetus and sex selection, or render services to any of them, after the commencement of the Pre-natal Diagnostic Techniques (Regulation and Prevention of Misuse) Amendment Act, 2002 unless such Centre, Laboratory or Clinic is duly registered under the Act.

(2) Every application for registration under sub-section (1), shall be made to the Appropriate Authority in such form and in such manner and shall be accompanied by such fees as may be prescribed.

(3) Every Genetic Counseling Centre, Genetic Laboratory or Genetic Clinic engaged, either partly or exclusively, in Counseling or conducting pre-natal diagnostic techniques for any of the purposes mentioned in section 4, immediately before the commencement of this Act, shall apply for registration within sixty days from the date of such commencement.

(4) Subject to the provisions of section 6, every Genetic Counseling Centre, Genetic Laboratory or Genetic Clinic engaged in Counseling or conducting pre-natal diagnostic techniques shall cease to conduct any such Counseling or technique on the expiry of six months from the date of commencement of this Act unless such Centre, Laboratory or Clinic has applied for registration and is so registered separately or jointly or till such application is disposed of, whichever is earlier.

(5) No Genetic Counseling Centre, Genetic Laboratroy or Genetic Clinic shall be registered under this Act unless the Appropriate Authority is satisfied that such Centre, Laboratory or Clinic is

in a position to provide such facilities, maintain such equipment and standards as may be prescribed.

Comments– No Genetic Counseling Centre, Genetic Laboratory or Genetic Clinic, including clinic, laboratory or centre having ultrasound or imaging machine or scanner or any other technology capable of undertaking determination of sex of foetus and sex selection can be opened unless it is duly registered under the Act.

19. Certificate of registration–

(1) The Appropriate Authority shall, after holding an inquiry and after satisfying itself that the applicant has complied with all the requirements of this Act and the rules made there under and having regard to the advice of the Advisory Committee in this behalf, grant a certificate of registration in the prescribed form jointly or separately to the Genetic Counseling Centre, Genetic Laboratory or Genetic Clinic, as the case may be.

(2) If, after the inquiry and after giving an opportunity of being heard to the applicant and having regard to the advice of the Advisory Committee, the Appropriate Authority is satisfied that the applicant has not complied with the requirements of this Act or the rules, it shall, for reasons to be recorded in writing, reject the application for registration.

(3) Every certificate of registration shall be renewed in such manner and after such period and on payment of such fees as may be prescribed.

(4) The certificate of registration shall be displayed by the registered Genetic Counseling Centre, Genetic Laboratory or Genetic Clinic in a conspicuous place at its place of business.

20. Cancellation or suspension of registration–

(1) The Appropriate Authority may *suo moto*, or on complaint, issue a notice to the Genetic Counseling Centre, Genetic Laboratory or Genetic Clinic to show cause why its registration should not be suspended or cancelled for the reasons mentioned in the notice.

(2) If, after giving a reasonable opportunity of being heard to the Genetic Counseling Centre, Genetic Laboratory or Genetic Clinic and having regard to the advice of the Advisory

Committee, the Appropriate Authority is satisfied that there has been a breach of the provisions of this Act or the rules, it may, without prejudice to any criminal action that it may take against such Centre, Laboratory or Clinic, suspend its registration for such period as it may think fit or cancel its registration, as the case may be.

(3) Notwithstanding anything contained in sub-sections (1) and (2), if the Appropriate Authority is of the opinion that it is necessary or expedient so to do in the public interest, it may, for reasons to be recorded in writing, suspend the registration of any Genetic Counseling Centre, Genetic Laboratory or Genetic Clinic without issuing any such notice referred to in sub-section (1).

21. Appeal–The Genetic Counseling Centre, Genetic Laboratory or Genetic Clinic may, within thirty days from the date of receipt of the order of suspension or cancellation of registration passed by the Appropriate Authority under section 20, prefer an appeal against such order to–

(i) the Central Government, where the appeal is against the order of the Central Appropriate Authority; and

(ii) the Stab; Government, where the appeal is against the order of the State Appropriate Authority, in the prescribed manner.

(VII) OFFENCES AND PENALTIES

[29]22. Prohibition of advertisement relating to pre-conception and pre-natal determination of sex and punishment for contravention–

(1) No person, organization, Genetic Counseling Centre, Genetic Laboratory or Genetic Clinic, including Clinic, Laboratory or Centre having ultrasound machine or imaging machine or scanner or any other technology capable of undertaking determination of sex of foetus or sex selection shall issue, publish, distribute, communicate or cause to be issued, published, distributed or communicated any advertisement, in any form, including internet, regarding facilities of prenatal determination of sex or sex selection before conception available at such Centre, Laboratory, Clinic or at any other place.

(2) No person or organisation including Genetic Counseling Centre,

Genetic Laboratory or Genetic Clinic shall issue, publish, distribute, communicate or cause to be issued, published, distributed or communicated any advertisement in any manner regarding pre-natal determination or pre-conception selection of sex by any means whatsoever, scientific or otherwise.

(3) Any person who contravenes the provisions of sub-section (1) or subsection (2) shall be punishable with imprisonment for a term which may extend to three years and with fine which may extend to ten thousand rupees.

Explanation-For the purposes of this section, "advertisement" includes any notice, circular, label, wrapper or any other document including advertisement through internet or any other media in electronic or print form and also includes any visible representation made by means of any hoarding, wall-painting, signal, light, sound, smoke or gas.

Comments– Advertisement relating to pre-conception and pre-natal determination of a sex or sex selection is prohibited. Contravention is punishable with imprisonment upto three years and with fine upto ten thousand rupees.

23. Offences and penalties–

(1) Any medical geneticist, gynaecologist, registered medical practitioner or any person who owns a Genetic Counseling Centre, a Genetic Laboratory or a Genetic Clinic or is employed in such a Centre, Laboratory or Clinic and renders his professional or technical services to or at such a Centre, Laboratory or Clinic, whether on an honorary basis or otherwise, and who contravenes any of the provisions of this Act or rules made thereunder shall be punishable with imprisonment for a term which may extend to three years and with fine which may extend to ten thousand rupees and on any subsequent conviction, with imprisonment which may extend to five years and with fine which may extend to fifty thousand rupees.

[30](2) The name of the registered medical practitioner shall be reported by the Appropriate Authority to the State Medical Council concerned for taking necessary action including suspension of the registration if the charges are framed by the court and till the case is disposed of and on conviction for removal of his name from the register of the Council for a period of five years for the first offence and permanently for the subsequent offence.

(3) Any person who seeks the aid of any Genetic Counseling Centre, Genetic Laboratory, Genetic Clinic or ultrasound clinic or imaging clinic or of a medical geneticist, gynaecologist, sonologist or imaging specialist or registered medical practitioner or any other person for sex selection or for conducting pre-natal diagnostic techniques on any pregnant woman for the purposes other than those specified in sub-section (2) of section 4, he shall be punishable with imprisonment for a term which may extend to three years and with fine which may extend to fifty thousand rupees for the first offence and for any subsequent offence with imprisonment which may extend to five years and with fine which may extend to one lakh rupees.

(4) For the removal of doubts, it is hereby provided, that the provisions of sub-section (3) shall not apply to the woman who was compelled to undergo such diagnostic techniques or such selection.

Comments– Any medical geneticist, gynaecologist, registered medical practitioner or any person who owns a Genetic Counseling Centre, a Genetic Laboratory or a Genetic Clinic or is employed therein and renders his professional or technical services there, whether on an honorary basis or other wise and who contravenes any of the provisions of the Act or rules made there under shall be punishable with imprisonment upto three years and with fine upto ten thousand rupees and on any subsequent conviction, with imprisonment upto five years and with fine upto fifty thousand rupees. The name of the registered medical practitioner shall be reported to the State Medical Council concerned for taking necessary action. If any person seeks aid for sex selection or for conducting pre-natal diagnostic techniques on any pregnant woman, he shall be punishable with imprisonment upto three years and with fine upto fifty thousand rupees for the first offence and for any subsequent offence, with imprisonment upto five years and with fine upto one lakh rupees.

[31]24. **Presumption in the case of conduct of pre-natal diagnostic techniques–** Notwithstanding anything contained in the Indian Evidence Act, 1872, the court shall presume unless the contrary is proved that the pregnant woman was compelled by her husband or any other relative, as the case may be, to undergo pre-

natal diagnostic technique for the purposes other than those specified in sub-section (2) of section 4 and such person shall be liable for abetment of offence under sub-section (3) of section 23 and shall be punishable for the offence specified under that section.

25. Penalty for contravention of the provisions of the Act or rules for which no specific punishment is provided–Whoever contravenes any of the provisions of this Act or any rules made there under, for which no penalty has been elsewhere provided in this Act, shall be punishable with imprisonment for a term which may extend to three months or with fine, which may extend to one thousand rupees or with both and in the case of continuing contravention with an additional fine which may extend to five hundred rupees for every day during which such contravention continues after conviction for the first such contravention.

26. Offences by Companies–

(1) Where any offence, punishable under this Act has been committed by a company, every person who, at the time the offence was committed was in charge of, and was responsible to the company for the conduct of the business of the company, as well as the company, shall be deemed to be guilty of the offence and shall be liable to be proceeded against and punished accordingly:

Provided that nothing contained in this sub-section shall render any such person liable to any punishment, if he proves that the offence was committed without his knowledge or that he had exercised all due diligence to prevent the commission of such offence.

(2) Notwithstanding anything contained in sub-section (1), where any offence punishable under this Act has been committed by a company and it is proved that the offence has been committed with the consent or connivance of, or is attributable to any neglect on the part of, any director, manager, secretary or other officer of the company, such director, manager, secretary or other officer shall also be deemed to be guilty of that offence and shall be liable to be proceeded against and punished "accordingly.

Explanation– For the purposes of this section, –

(a) "company" means anybody corporate and includes a firm or other association of individuals, and

(b) "director", in relation to a firm, means a partner in the firm.

27. Offence to be cognizable, non-bailable and non-compoundable–

Every offence under this Act shall be cognizable, non-bailable and non-compoundable.

28. Cognizance of offences–

(1) No court shall take cognizance of an offence under this Act except on a complaint made by–

  (a) the Appropriate Authority concerned, or any officer authorised in this behalf by Central Government or State Government, as the case may be, or the Appropriate Authority; or

  (b) a person who has given notice of not less than[32] in the manner prescribed, to the Appropriate Authority, of the alleged offence and of his intention to make a complaint to the court.

Explanation–For the purpose of this clause, "person" includes a social organisation.

(2) No court other than that of a Metropolitan Magistrate or a Judicial Magistrate of the first class shall try any offence punishable under this Act.

(3) Where a complaint has been made under clause (b) of sub-section (1), the court may, on demand by such person, direct the Appropriate Authority to make available copies of the relevant records in its possession to such person.

(VIII) MISCELLANEOUS

29. Maintenance of records–

(1) All records, charts, forms, reports, consent letters and all the documents required to be maintained under this Act and the rules shall be preserved for a period of two years or for such period as may be prescribed:

Provided that, if any criminal or other proceedings are instituted against any Genetic Counseling Centre, Genetic Laboratory or

Genetic Clinic, the records and all other documents of such Centre, Laboratory or Clinic shall be preserved till the final disposal of such proceedings.

(2) All such records shall, at all reasonable times, be made available for inspection to the Appropriate Authority or to any other person authorised by the Appropriate Authority in this behalf.

30. Power to search and seize records, etc.[33]–

(1) If the Appropriate Authority has reason to believe that an offence under this Act has been or is being committed at any Genetic Counseling Centre, Genetic Laboratory, Genetic Clinic or any other place, such Authority or any officer authorised in this behalf may, subject to such rules as may be prescribed, enter and search at all reasonable times with such assistance, if any, as such Authority or officer considers necessary, such Genetic Counseling Centre, Genetic Laboratory, Genetic Clinic or any other place and examine any record, register, document book, pamphlet, advertisement or any other material object found therein and seize and seal the same if such Authority or officer has reason to believe that it may furnish evidence of the commission of an offence punishable under this Act.

(2) The provisions of the Code of Criminal Procedure, 1973 (2 of 1974) relating to searches and seizures shall, so far as may be, apply to every search or seizure; made under this Act.

31. Protection of action taken in good faith– No suit, prosecution or other legal proceeding shall lie against the Central or the State Government or the Appropriate Authority or any officer authorised by the Central or State Government or by the Authority for anything which is in good faith, done or intended to be done in pursuance of the provisions of this Act.

[34]**31A. Removal of difficulties–**

(1) If any difficulty arises in giving effect to the provisions of the Pre-natal Diagnostic Techniques (Regulation and Prevention of Misuse) Amendment Act, 2002, the Central Government may, by order published in the Official Gazette, make such provisions not inconsistent with the provisions of the said Act as appear to it to be necessary or expedient for removing the difficulty:

Provided that no order shall be made under this section after the expiry of a period of three years from the date of commencement of the Pre-natal Diagnostic techniques (Regulation and Prevention of Misuse) Amendment Act, 2002.

(2) Every order made under this section shall be laid, as soon as may be after it is made, before each House of Parliament.

32. Power to make rules–

(1) The Central Government may make rules for carrying out the provisions of this Act.

(2) In particular, and without prejudice to the generality of the foregoing power, such rules may provide for–

[35](i) the minimum qualifications for persons employed at a registered Genetic Counseling Centre, Genetic Laboratory or Genetic Clinic under clause (2) of section 3;

(ia) the manner in which the person conducting ultrasonography on a pregnant woman shall keep record thereof in the clinic under the proviso to sub-section (3) of section 4;

(ii) the form in which consent of a pregnant woman has to be obtained under section 5;

(iii) the procedure to be followed by the members of the Central Supervisory Board in the discharge of their functions under subsection (4) of section 8;

(iv) allowances for members other than ex-officio members admissible under sub-section (5) of section 9;

(iva) code of conduct to be observed by persons working at Genetic Counseling Centres, Genetic Laboratories and Genetic Clinics to be laid down by the Central Supervisory Board under clause (iv) of section 16;[36]

(ivb) the manner in which reports shall be furnished by the State and Union Territory Supervisory Boards to the Board and the Central Government in respect of various activities undertaken in the State under the Act under clause (iv) of sub-section (1) of section 16A;

(ivc) empowering the Appropriate Authority in any other matter under clause (d) of section 17A.

(v) the period intervening between any two meetings of the Advisory Committee under the proviso to sub-section (8) of section 17;

(vi) the terms and conditions subject to which a person may be appointed to the Advisory Committee and the procedure to be followed by such Committee under sub-section (9) of section 1;

(vii) the form and manner in which an application shall be made for registration and the fee payable thereof under sub-section (2) of section 18;

(viii) the facilities to be provided, equipment and other standards to be maintained by the Genetic Counseling Centre, Genetic Laboratory or Genetic Clinic under sub-section (5) of section 18;

(ix) the form in which a certificate of registration shall be issued under sub-section (1) of section 19;

(x) the manner in which and the period after which a certificate of registration shall be renewed and the fee payable for such renewal under sub-section (3) of section 19;

(xi) the manner in which an appeal may be preferred under section 21;

(xii) the period up to which records, charts, etc., shall be preserved under sub-section (1) of section 29;

(xiii) the manner in which the seizure of documents, records, objects, etc., shall be made and the manner in which seizure list shall be prepared and delivered to the person from whose custody such documents, records or objects were seized under sub-section (1) of section 30;

(xiv) any other matter that is required to be, or may be, prescribed.

33. Power to make regulations–The Board may, with the previous sanction of the Central Government, by notification in the Official Gazette, make regulations not inconsistent with the provisions of this Act and the rules made there under to provide for–

(a) the time and place of the meetings of the Board and the procedure to be followed for the transaction of business at such meetings and the number of members which shall form the quorum under sub-section (1) of section 9;

(b) the manner in which a person may be temporarily associated with the Board under sub-section (1) of section 11;

(c) the method of appointment, the conditions of service and the scales of pay and allowances of the officer and other employees of the Board appointed under section 12;

(d) generally for the efficient conduct of the affairs of the Board.

34. Rules and regulations to be laid before Parliament–Every rule and every regulation made under this Act shall be laid, as soon as may be after it is made, before each House of Parliament, while it is in session, for a total period of thirty days which may be comprised in one session or in two or more successive sessions, and if, before the expiry of the session immediately following the session or the successive sessions aforesaid, both Houses agree in making any modification in the rule or regulation or both Houses agree that the rule or regulation should not be-made, the rule or regulation shall thereafter have effect only in such modified form or be of no effect, as the case may be; so, however, that any such modification or annulment shall be without prejudice to the validity of anything previously done under that rule or regulation.

NOTES

1. Subs, by Act 14 of 2003, sec. 1, for the long title (w.e.f. 14-2-2003) (see Annexe).
2. Subs, by Act 14 of 2003, feec. 3, for "the Pre-natal Diagnostic Techniques (Regulation and Prevention of Misuse)" (w.e.f. 14-2-2003).
3. Came into force on 1-1-1996, vide S.O. 990(E), dated 20th December, 1995, published in the Gazette of India, Extra., Pt. II, Sec. 3 (ii), dated 21st December, 1995.
4. Ins. by Act 14 of 2003, sec. 4 (w.e.f. 14-2-2003).
5. by Act 14 of 2003, sec. 4 (k.e.f. 14-2-2003)
6. Subs, by Act 14 of 2003, sec. 4 for clause (g) (w.e.f. 14-2-2003) (see Annexe).

7. Subs, by Act 14 of 2003, sec. 4 for clause (i) (w.e.f. 14-2-2003) (see Annexe).
8. Subs, by Act 14 of 2003, sec. 4 for clause (k) (w.e.f. 14-2-2003) (see Annexe).
9. Ins. by Act 14 of 2003, sec. 4 (w.e.f. 14-2-2003).
10. Subs, by Act 14 of 2003, sec. 5, for clause (2) (w.e.f. 14-2-2003) (see Annexe).
11. Ins. by Act 14 of 2003, sec 6 (w.e.f. 14-2-2003).
12. Supervisory Board has specified as follows: "any other indication of possible genetic disease/anomaly in the foetus such as sporadic genetic disease in the couple, a positive screening test for carrier status or positive screening test for genetic, disease/congenital anomaly in pregnancy etc." (Vide S.O. 189(E), dated 12th February, 2004).
13. Subs, by Act 14 of 2003, sec. 7, for clauses (3) and (4) (w.e.f. 14-2-2003) (see Annexe).
14. Subs, by Act 14 of 2003, Sec. 8, for sub-section (2) (w.e.f. 14-2-2003) (see Annexe).
15. Ins. by Act 14 of 2003, sec. 9 (w.e.f. 14-2-2003).
16. Subs, by Act H of 2003, sec. 10, for clause (c) (w.e.f. 14-2-2003) (see Annexe).
17. Subs, by Act 14 of 2003, sec. 10, for sub-clause (ii) (w.e.f. 14-2-2003) (seeAnnexe).
18. The word "and" omitted by Act 32 of 2001, see. 2 (w.e.f. 3-9-2001).
19. Ins. by Act 32 of 2001, sec. 2 (w.e.f. 3-9-2001).
20. Subs. Act 14 of 2003, sec. 11, for clause (f) (w.e.f. 14-2-2003) (see Annexe).
21. Ins. by Act 14 of 2003, set. 12 (w.e.f. 14-2-2003).
22. Subs, by Act 14 of 2003, sec. 13, for section 16 (w.e.f. 14-2-2003) (seeAnnexe).
23. Ins. by Act 14 of 2003, sec. 14 (w.e.f. 14-2-2003).
24. Subs, by Act 14 of 2003, sec. 15, for clause (a) (w.e.f. 14-2-2003) (see Annexe).

25. Ins. by Act 14 of 2003, sec. 15 (w.e.f. 14-2-2003).
26. Subs, by Act 14 of 2003, sec. 15, for sub-section (7) (w.e.f. 14-2-2003) (see Annexe).
27. Ins. by Act 14 of 2003, sec. 16 (w.e.f. 14-2-2003).
28. Subs, by Act 14 of 2003, sue. 17, for sub-section (1) (w.e.f. 14-2-2003) (see Annexe).
29. Subs, by Act 14 of 2003, sec. 18, for section 22 (w.e.f. 14-2-2003) (see Annexe).
30. Subs, by Act 14 of 2003, sec. 19, for sub-sections (2) and (3) (w.e.f. 14-2-2003) (see Annexe).
31. Subs, by Act 14 of 2003, sec. 20, for section 24 (w.e.f. 14-2-2003) (see Annexe).
32. Subs, by Act 14 of 2003, sec. 21, for "thirty days" (w.e.f. 14-2-2003).
33. Subs, by Act 14 of 2003, jiec. 22, for sub-section (1) (w.e.f. 14-2-2003) (see Annexe).
34. Ins. by Act 14 of 2003, sec. 23 (w.e.f. 14-2-2003).
35. Subs, by Act 14 of 2003, sec. 24, for clause (i) (w.e.f. 14-2-2003) (see Annexe).
36. Ins. by Act 14 of 2003, sec 24 (w.e.f. 14-2-2003).

ANNEXURE – II

THE PRE-CONCEPTION AND PRE-NATAL DIAGNOSTIC TECHNIQUES (PROHIBITION OF SEX SELECTION) RULES, 1996[1]

In exercise of the powers conferred by section 32 of the Pre-natal Diagnostic Techniques (Regulation and Prevention of Misuse) Act, 1994 (57 of 1994), the Central Government hereby makes the following rules, namely:

1. Short title and commencement[2]–

(1) These rules may be called the Pre-conception and Pre-natal Diagnostic Techniques (Prohibition of Sex Selection) Rules, 1996.

(2) They shall come into force on the date of their publication in the Official Gazette.

2. Definitions–

In these rules, unless the context otherwise requires, –

(a) "Act" means The Pre-natal Diagnostic Techniques (Regulation and Prevention of Misuse) Act, 1994 (57 of 1994);

(b) "employee" means a person working in or employed by a Genetic Counseling Centre, a Genetic Laboratory or a Genetic and includes those working on part-time, contractual, consultancy, honorary or on any other basis;

(c) "Form" means a form appended to these rules;

(d) xxxx[3]

(e) "section" means a section of the Act;

(f) words aid expressions used herein and not defined in these rules but defined in the Act, shall have the meanings, respectively, assigned to them in the Act.

The qualification of the employees, the requirement of equipment etc. for a Genetic Counseling Centre, Genetic Laboratory, Ultrasound Clinic and Imaging Centre shall be as under:

(1) Any person being or employing–

(i) a gynaecologist or a paediatrician having six months experience or four weeks training in genetic Counseling, or

(ii) a medical geneticist,

having adequate space and educational charts/models/equipments for carrying out genetic Counseling may set up a genetic Counseling centre and get it registered as a genetic Counseling centre.

(2) (a) Any person having adequate space and being or employing

(i) a Medical Geneticist and

(ii) a laboratory technician, having a B.Sc. degree in Biological Sciences or a degree or diploma in medical laboratory course with at least one year experience in conducting appropriate prenatal diagnostic techniques, tests or procedures may set up a Genetic Laboratory.

(b) Such laboratory should have or acquire such of the following equipments as may be necessary for carrying out chromosomal studies, bio-chemical studies and molecular studies: -

(i) *Chromosomal studies:*

(1) Laminar flow hood with ultraviolet and fluorescent light or other suitable culture hood.

(2) Photo-microscope with fluorescent source of light.

(3) Inverted microscope.

(4) Incubator and oven.

(5) Carbon dioxide incubator or closed system with 5% CO2 atmosphere.

(6) Autoclave.

(7) Refrigerator.

(8) Water bath.

(9) Centrifuge.

(10) Vortex mixer.

(11) Magnetic stirrer.

(12) pH Meter.

(13) A sensitive balance (preferably electronic) with sensitivity of 0.1 milligram.

(14) Double distillation apparatus (glass).

(15) Such other equipments as may be necessary,

(ii) ***Biochemical studies:***

(requirements according to tests to be carried out)

(1) Laminar flow hood with ultraviolet and fluorescent light or other suitable culture hood.

(2) Inverted microscope.

(3) Incubator and oven.

(4) Carbon dioxide incubator or closed system with 5% CO_2 atmosphere.

(5) Autoclave.

(6) Refrigerator.

(7) Water bath.

(8) Centrifuge.

(9) Electrophoresis apparatus and power supply.

(10) Chromatography chamber.

(11) Spectro-photometer and Elisa reader or Radio-immunoassay system (with gamma beta counter) or fluorometer for various biochemical tests.

(12) Vortex mixer.

(13) Magnetic stirrer

(14) pH meter.

(15) A sensitive balance (preferable electronic) with sensitivity of 0.1 milligram.

(16) Double distillation apparatus (glass).

(17) Liquid nitrogen tank.

(18) Such other equipments as may be necessary,

(iii) ***Molecular studies:***

(1) Inverted microscope.

(2) Incubator.

(3) Oven.

(4) Autoclave.

(5) Refrigerators (4 degree and minus 20 degree Centigrade).

(6) Water bath.

(7) Micro centrifuge.

(8) Electrophoresis apparatus and power supply.
(9) Vertex mixer.
(10) Magnetic stirrer
(11) pH meter.
(12) A sensitive balance (preferably electronic) with sensitivity of 0.1 illigram.
(13) Double distillation apparatus (glass)
(14) P.C.R. machine
(15) Refrigerated centrifuge.
(16) U.V. Illuminator with photographic attachment or other documentation system.
(17) Precision micropipettes.
(18) Such other equipments as may be necessary.

(3) (1) Any person having adequate space and being or employing–

(a) Gynaecologist having experience of performing at least 20 procedures in chorionic villi aspirations per vagina or per abdomen, chorionic villi biopsy, amniocentesis, cordocen-tesis foetoscopy, foetal skin or organ biopsy or foetal blood sampling etc., under supervision of an experienced gynaecologist in these fields, or

(b) a Sonologist, Imaging Specialist, Radiologist or Registered Medical Practitioner having Post-Graduate degree or diploma or six months training or one year experience in sonography or image scanning, or

(c) A medical geneticist may set up a genetic clinic/ultrasound clinic/imaging centre.

(2) The Genetic Clinic/ultrasound clinic/imaging centre should have or acquire such of the following equipments, as may be necessary for carrying out the tests or procedures–

(a) Equipment and accessories necessary for carrying out clinical examination by an obstetrician or gynaecologist.

(b) An ultra-sonography machine including mobile ultrasound machine, imaging machine or any other equipment capable of conducting foetal ultrasonography.

(c) Appropriate catheters and equipment for carrying out chorionic villi aspirations per vagina or per abdomen.

(d) Appropriate sterile needles for amniocentesis or cordocentesis.

(e) A suitable foetoscope with appropriate accessories for foetoscopy, foetal skin or organ biopsy or foetal blood sampling shall be optional.

(f) Equipment for dry and wet sterilization.

(g) Equipment for carrying out emergency procedures such as evacuation of uterus or resuscitation in case of need.

(h) Genetic works station.

[4]3A. Sale of ultrasound machines/imaging machines–

(1) No organization including a commercial organization or a person, including manufacturer, importer, dealer or supplier of ultrasound machines/ imaging machines or any other equipment, capable of detecting sex of foetus, shall sell, distribute, supply, rent, allow or authorize the use of any such machine or equipment in any manner, whether on payment or otherwise, to any Genetic Counseling Centre, Genetic Laboratory, Genetic Clinic, Ultrasound Clinic, Imaging Centre or any other body or person unless such Centre, Laboratory, Clinic, body or person is registered under the Act.

(2) The provider of such machine/equipment to any person/body registered under the Act shall send to the concerned State/Union Territory Appropriate Authority and to the Central Government, once in three months a list of those to whom the machine/equipment has been provided.

(3) Any organization or person, including manufacturer, importer, dealer or supplier of ultrasound machines/imaging machines or any other equipment capable of detecting sex of foetus selling, distributing, supplying or authorizing, in any manner, the use of any such machine or equipment to any Genetic Counseling Centre, Genetic Laboratory, Genetic Clinic, Ultrasound Clinic, Imaging Centre or any other body or person registered under the Act shall take an affidavit from such body or person purchasing or getting authorization for using such machine/equipment that the machine/equipment shall not be used for

detection of sex of foetus or selection of sex before after conception.

4. Registration of Genetic Counseling Centre, Genetic Laboratory, Genetic Clinic–

(1) An application for registration shall be made to the Appropriate Authority, in duplicate, in Form A, duly accompanied by an affidavit containing–

   (i) an undertaking to the effect that the Genetic Centre/ Laboratory/ Clinic/ Ultrasound Clinic/ Imaging Centre/ Combination thereof, as the case may be, shall not conduct any test or procedure, by whatever name called, for selection of sex before or after conception or for detection of sex of foetus except for diseases specified in section 4 (2) nor shall the sex of foetus be disclosed to any body; and

   (ii) an undertaking to the effect that the Genetic Centre/ Laboratory/ Clinic/ Combination thereof, as the case may be, shall display prominently a notice that they do not conduct any technique, test or procedure etc., by whatever name called, for detection of sex of foetus or for selection of sex before or after conception.

(2) The Appropriate Authority, or any person in his office authorized in this behalf, shall acknowledge receipt of the application for registration, in the acknowledgement slip provided at the bottom of Form A, immediately if delivered at the office of the Appropriate Authority, or not later than the next working day if received by post.

5. Application Fee[5] –

(1) Every application for registration under rule 4 shall be accompanied by an application fee of–

   (a) Rs. 3000.00 for Genetic Counseling Centre, Genetic Laboratory, Genetic Clinic, Ultrasound Clinic or Imaging Centre.

   (b) Rs. 4000.00 for an institute, hospital, nursing home, or any place providing jointly the service of a Genetic Counseling Centre, Genetic Laboratory and Genetic

Clinic, Ultrasound Clinic or Imaging Centre or any combination thereof:

Provided that if an application for registration of any Genetic Clinic/ Laboratory/Centre, etc., has been rejected by the Appropriate Authority, no fee shall be required to be paid on re-submission of the application by the applicant for the same body within 90 days of rejection. Provided further that any subsequent application shall be accompanied with the prescribed fee. Application fee once paid will not be refunded.

(2) The application fee shall be paid by a demand draft drawn in favour of the Appropriate Authority, on any scheduled bank payable at the headquarters of the Appropriate Authority concerned. The fees collected by the Appropriate Authorities for registration of Genetic Counseling Centre, Genetic Laboratory, Genetic Clinic, Ultrasound Clinic and Imaging Centre or any other body or person under sub-rule (1), shall be deposited by the Appropriate Authority concerned in a bank account opened in the name of the official designation of the Appropriate Authority concerned and shall be utilized by the Appropriate Authority in connection with the activities connected with implementation of the provisions of the Act and these rules.

6. Certificate of Registration

(1) The Appropriate Authority shall, after making such enquiry and after satisfying itself that the applicant has complied with all the requirements, place the application before the Advisory Committee for its advice.

(2) Having regard to the advice of the Advisory Committee the Appropriate Authority shall grant a certificate of registration, in duplicate, in Form B to the applicant. One copy of the certificate of registration shall be displayed by the registered Genetic Counseling Centre, Genetic Laboratory, Genetic Clinic, Ultrasound Clinic or Imaging Centre at a conspicuous place at its place of business:

Provided that the Appropriate Authority may grant a certificate of registration to a Genetic Laboratory or a Genetic Clinic Ultrasound clinic or Imaging Centre to conduct one or more specified pre-natal diagnostic tests or procedures, depending on the availability of place, equipment and qualified employees, and standards maintained by such laboratory or clinic.

(3) If, after enquiry and after giving an opportunity of being heard to the applicant and having regard to the advice of the Advisory Committee, the Appropriate Authority is satisfied that the applicant has not complied with the requirements of the Act and these rules, it shall, for the reasons to be recorded in writing, reject the application for registration and communicate such rejection to the applicant as specified in Form C.

(4) An enquiry under sub-rule (1), including inspection at the premises of the[6] Genetic Counseling Centre, Genetic Laboratory Genetic Clinic, Ultrasound Clinic or Imaging Centre, shall, be carried out only after due notice is given to the applicant by the Appropriate Authority.

(5) Grant of certificate of registration or rejection of application for registration shall be communicated to the applicant as specified in Form B or Form C, as the case may be, within a period of ninety days from the date of receipt of application for registration.

(6) The certificate of registration shall be non-transferable. In the event of change of ownership or change of management or on ceasing to function as a Genetic Counseling Centre, Genetic Laboratory, Genetic Clinic, Ultrasound Clinic or Imaging Centre, both copies of the certificate of registration shall be surrendered to the Appropriate Authority.

(7) In the event of change of ownership or change of management of the Genetic Counseling Centre, Genetic Laboratory, Genetic Clinic, Ultrasound Clinic or Imaging Centre, the new owner or manager of such Centre, Laboratory or Clinic shall apply afresh for grant of certificate of registration.

7. Validity of registration–

Every certificate of registration shall be valid for a period of five years from the date of its issue.

8. Renewal of registration–

(1) An application for renewal of certificate of registration shall be made in duplicate in Form A, to the Appropriate Authority

thirty days before the date of expiry of the certificate of registration. Acknowledgement of receipt of such application shall be issued by the Appropriate Authority in the manner specified in sub-rule (2) of rule 4.

(2) The Appropriate Authority shall, after holding an enquiry and after satisfying itself that the applicant has complied with all the requirements of the Act and these rules and having regard to the advice of the Advisory Committee in this behalf, renew the certificate of registration, as specified in Form B, for a further period of five years from the date of expiry of the certificate of registration earlier granted.

(3) If, after enquiry and after giving an opportunity of being heard to the applicant and having regard to the advice of the Advisory Committee, the Appropriate Authority is satisfied that the applicant has not complied with the requirements of the Act and these rules, it shall, for reasons to be recorded in writing, reject the application for renewal of certificate of registration and communicate such rejection to the applicant, as specified in Form C.

(4) The fees payable for renewal of certificate registration shall be one half of the fees provided in sub-rule (1) of rule 5.

(5) On receipt of the renewed certificate of registration in duplicate or on receipt of communication of rejection of application for renewal, both copies of the earlier certificate of registration shall be surrendered immediately to the Appropriate Authority by the Genetic Counseling Centre, Genetic Laboratory, Genetic Clinic, Ultrasound Clinic or Imaging Centre.

(6) In the event of failure of the Appropriate Authority to renew the certificate of registration or to communicate rejection of application for renewal of registration within a period of ninety days from the date of receipt of application for renewal of registration, the certificate of registration shall be deemed to have been renewed.

9. Maintenance and preservation of records[7]–

(1) Every Genetic Counseling Centre, Genetic Laboratory, Genetic Clinic, Ultrasound Clinic and Imaging Centre shall maintain a register showing, in serial order, the names and addresses of the men or women given genetic Counseling, subjected to pre-natal

diagnostic procedures or pre-natal diagnostic tests, the names of their spouse or fathers and the date on which they first reported for such Counseling, procedure or test.

(2) The record to be maintained by every Genetic Counseling Centre, in respect of each woman counseled shall be as specified in Form D.

(3)[8] The record to be maintained by every Genetic Laboratory, in respect of each man or woman subjected to any pre-natal diagnostic procedure/technique/test, shall be as specified in Form F.

(4) The record to be maintained by every Genetic Clinic, in respect of each man or woman subjected to any pre-natal diagnostic procedure/ technique/test, shall be as specified in Form F.

(5) The Appropriate Authority shall maintain a permanent record of applications for grant or renewal of certificate of registration as specified in Form H. Letters of intimation of every change of employee, place, address and equipment installed shall also be preserved as permanent records.

(6) All case related records, forms of consent, laboratory results, microscopic pictures, sonographic plates or slides, recommendations and letters shall be preserved by the[9] Genetic Counseling Centre, Genetic Laboratory, Genetic Clinic, Ultrasound Clinic or Imaging Centre for a period of two years from the date of completion of Counseling, pre-natal diagnostic procedure or pre-natal diagnostic test, as the case may be. In the event of any legal proceedings, the records shall be preserved till the final disposal of legal proceedings, or till the expiry of the said period of two years, whichever is later.

(7) In case where Genetic Counseling Centre or Genetic Laboratory or Genetic Clinic, Ultrasound Clinic or Imaging Centre maintains records on computer or other electronic equipment, a printed copy of the record shall be taken and preserved after authentication by a person responsible for such record.

(8) Every Genetic Counseling[10] Centre, Genetic Laboratory, Genetic Clinic, Ultrasound Clinic and Imaging Centre shall send a complete report in respect of all pre-conception or pregnancy related procedures/techniques/tests conducted by them in respect of each month by 5th day of the following month to the concerned Appropriate Authority.

10. Conditions for conducting pre-natal diagnostic procedures–

(1) Before conducting preimplantation genetic diagnosis, or any pre-natal diagnostic technique/test/procedure such as amniocentesis, chorionic villli biopsy, foetoscopy, foetal skin or organ biospsy or cordocentesis, written consent, as specified in Form G, in a language the person undergoing such procedure understands, shall be obtained from her/him:

Provided that where a Genetic Clinic has taken a sample of any body tissue or body fluid and sent it to a Genetic Laboratory for analysis or test, it shall not be necessary for the Genetic Laboratory to obtain a fresh consent in Form G.

(1A) Any person conducting ultrasonography/image scanning on a pregnant woman shall give a declaration on each report on ultrasonography/image scanning that he/she has neither detected nor disclosed the sex of foetus of the pregnant woman to anybody. The pregnant woman shall before undergoing ultrasonography/ image scanning declare that she does not want to know the sex of her foetus.

(2) All the State Governments and Union territories may issue translation of Form G in languages used in the State or Union Territory and where no official translation in a language understood by the pregnant woman is available, the Genetic Clinic may translate Form G into a language she understands.

11. Facilities for inspection

(1) Every Genetic Counseling Centre, Genetic Laboratory, Genetic Clinic, Ultrasound Clinic, Imaging Centre, nursing home, hospital, institute or any other place where any of the machines or equipments capable of performing any procedure, technique or pre-natal determination of sex or selection of sex before or after conception is used, shall afford all reasonable facilities for inspection of the place, equipment and records to the Appropriate Authority or to any other person authorized by the Appropriate Authority in this behalf for registration of such institutions, by whatever name called, under the Act, or for detection of misuse of such facilities or advertisement therefore or for selection of sex before or after conception or for detection/ disclosure of sex of foetus or for detection of cases of violation of the provisions of the Act in any other manner.

(2) The Appropriate Authority or the officer authorized by it may seal and seize any ultrasound machine, scanner or any other equipment, capable of detecting sex of foetus, used by any organisation if the organisation has not, got itself registered under the Act. These machines of the organisations may be released if such organisation pays penalty equal to five times of the registration fee to the Appropriate Authority concerned and give an undertaking that it shall not undertake detection of sex of foetus or selection of sex before or after conception.

12. Procedure for search and seizure[11] –

(1) The Appropriate Authority or any officer authorised in this behalf may enter and search at all reasonable times any Genetic Counseling Centre, Genetic Laboratory, Genetic Clinic, Imaging Centre or Ultrasound Clinic in the presence of two or more independent witnesses for the purposes of search and examination of any record, register, document, book, pamphlet, advertisement, or any other material object found therein and seal and seize the same if there is reason to believe that it may furnish evidence of commission of an offence punishable under the Act.

Explanation– In these Rules-

(i) 'Genetic Laboratory/Genetic Clinic/Genetic Counseling Centre' would include an Ultrasound Centre/Imaging Centre/nursing home/hospital/institute or any other place, by whatever name called, where any of the machines or equipments capable of selection of sex before or after conception or performing any procedure technique or test for pre-natal detection of sex of foetus, is used;

(ii) material object would include records, machines and equipments; and

(iii) 'seize' and 'seizure' would include 'seal' and 'sealing' respectively.

(2) A list of any document, record, register, book, pamphlet, advertisement or any other material object found in the 'Genetic Counseling Centre, Genetic Laboratory, Genetic Clinic, Ultrasound Clinic and Imaging Centre and seized shall be prepared in duplicate at the place of effecting the seizure, both

copies of such list shall be signed on every page by the Appropriate Authority or the officer authorized in this behalf and by the witnesses to the seizure:

Provided that the list may be prepared, in the presence of the witnesses, at a place other than the place of seizure if, for reasons to be recorded in writing, it is not practicable to make the list at the place of effecting the seizure.

(3) One copy of the list referred to in sub-rule (2) shall be handed over, under acknowledgement, to the person from whose custody the document, record, register, book, pamphlet advertisement or any other material object have been seized:

Provided that a copy of the list of such document, record, register, book, pamphlet, advertisement or other material object seized may be delivered under acknowledgement, or sent by registered post to the owner or manager of the Genetic Counseling Centre, Genetic Laboratory, Genetic Clinic, Ultrasound Clinic or Imaging Centre, if no person acknowledging custody of the document, record, register, book, pamphlet, advertisement or other material object seized is available at the place of effecting the seizure.

(4) If any material object seized is perishable in nature, the Appropriate Authority, or the officer authorised in this behalf shall make arrangements promptly for sealing, identification and preservation of the material object and also convey it to a facility for analysis or test, if analysis or test be required:

Provided that the refrigerator or other equipment used by the Genetic Counseling Centre, Genetic Laboratory, Genetic Clinic, Ultrasound Clinic and Imaging Centre for preserving such perishable material object may be sealed until such time as arrangements can be made for safe removal of such perishable material object and in such eventuality, mention of keeping the material object seized, on the premises of the Genetic Counseling Centre, Genetic Laboratory or Genetic Clinic shall be made in the list of seizure.

(5) In the case of non-completion of search and seizure operation, the Appropriate Authority or the officer authorized in this behalf may make arrangements, by way of mounting a guard or sealing of the premises of the 'Genetic Counseling Centre, Genetic Laboratory, Genetic Clinic, Ultrasound Clinic and Imaging

Centre, for safe keeping, listing and removal of documents, records, book or any other material object to be seized, and to prevent any tampering with such documents, records, books or any other material object.

13. Intimation of changes in employees, place or equipment.—

Every [12]Genetic Counseling Centre, Genetic Laboratory, Genetic Clinic, Ultrasound Clinic and Imaging Centre shall intimate every change of employee, place, address and equipment installed, to the Appropriate Authority within a period of thirty days of such change.

14. Conditions tor analysis or test and pre-natal diagnostic procedures–

(1) No Genetic Laboratory shall accept for analysis or test any sample, unless referred to it by a Genetic Clinic.

(2) Every pre-natal diagnostic procedure shall invariably be immediately preceded by locating the foetus and placenta through ultrasonography, and the pre-natal diagnostic procedure shall be done under direct ultrasonographic monitoring so as to prevent any damage to the foetus and placenta.

15. Meetings of the Advisory Committees–

The intervening period between any two meetings of Advisory Commitees constituted under subsection (5) of section 17 to advise the Appropriate Authority shall not exceed sixty days.

16. Allowances to members of the Central Supervisory Board–

(1) The ex-officio members, and other Central and State Government officers appointed to the Board will be entitled to Travelling Allowance and Daily Allowance for attending the meetings of the Board as per the Travelling Allowances rules applicable to them.

(2) The non-official members appointed to, and Members of Parliament elected to the Board will be entitled to Travelling Allowance and Daily Allowance or attending the meetings of

the Board as admissible to non-official and Members of Parliament as the case may be, under the Travelling Allowances rules of the Central Government.

17. Public Information–

(1) Every [13]Genetic Counseling Centre, Genetic Laboratory, Genetic Clinic, Ultrasound Clinic and Imaging Centre] shall prominently display on its premises a notice in English and in the local language or languages for the information of the public, to the effect that disclosure of the sex of the foetus is prohibited under law.

(2) At least one copy each of the Act and these rules shall be available on the premises of every Genetic Counseling, Centre, Genetic Laboratory, Genetic Clinic, Ultrasound Clinic and Imaging Centre, and shall be made available to the client on demand for perusal.

(3) The Appropriate Authority, the Central Government, the State Government, and the Government/Administration of the Union Territory may publish periodically lists of registered 'Genetic Counseling Centres, Genetic Laboratories, Genetic Clinics, Ultrasound Clinics and Imaging Centres and findings from the reports and other information in their possession, for the information of the public and for use by the experts in the field.

18. Code of Conduct to be observed by persons working at Genetic Counseling Centres, Genetic Laboratories, Genetic Clinics, Ultrasound Clinics, Imaging Centres, etc.–

All persons including the owners, employee or any other persons associated with Genetic Counseling Centres, Genetic Laboratories, Genetic Clinics, Ultrasound Clinics, Imaging Centres registered under the Act/these rules shall–

(i) not conduct or associate with, or help in carrying out detection or disclosure of sex of foetus in any manner;

(ii) not employ or cause to be employed any person not possessing qualifications necessary for carrying out pre-natal diagnostic techniques/procedures, tests including ultra-sonography;

(iii) not conduct or cause to be conducted or aid in conducting by him-self or through any other person any techniques or procedure for selection of sex before or after conception or for detection of sex of foetus except for the purposes specified in sub-section (2) of section 4 of the Act;

(iv) not conduct or cause to be conducted or aid in conducting by him-self or through any other person any techniques or test or procedure under the Act at a place other than a place registered under the Act/the rules;

(v) ensure that no provision of the Act and these Rules are violated in any manner;

(vi) ensure that the person conducting any techniques, test or proce-dure leading to detection of sex of foetus for purposes not covered under section 4 (2) of the Act or selection of sex before or after conception, is informed that such procedures lead to violation of the Act and the Rules which are punishable offences;

(vii) help the law enforcing agencies in bring to book the violators of the provisions of the Act and the Rules;

(viii) display his/her name and designation prominently on the dress worn by him/her;

(ix) write his/her name and designation in full under his/her signature;

(x) on no account conduct or allow/cause to be conducted female foeticide;

(xi) not commit any other act of professional misconduct.

[14]19. Appeals-

(1) Anybody aggrieved by the decision of the Appropriate Authority at sub-district level may appeal to the Appropriate Authority at district level within 30 days of the order of the sub-district level Appropriate Authority.

(2) Anybody aggrieved by the decision of the Appropriate Authority at district level may appeal to the Appropriate Authority at State/ UT level within 30 days of the order of the district level Appropriate Authority.

(3) Each appeal shall be disposed of by the District Appropriate Authority or by the State/Union Territory Appropriate Authority, as the case may be, within 60 days of its receipt.

(4) If an appeal is not made within the time as prescribed under sub-rule (1), (2) or (3), the Appropriate Authority under that sub-

rule may condone the delay in case he/she is satisfied that appellant was prevented for sufficient cause from making such appeal.

NOTES

1. Vide G.S.R. 1 (E), dated 1st January, 1996, published in the Gazette of India, Extra., Pt. II, Sue. 3 (i), dated 1st January, 1 996. + Now the Pre-conception and Pre-natal Diagnostic Techniques (Prohibition of Sex Selection) Act, 1994 (57 of 1994).
2. Subs, by G.S.R. 109 (E), dated 14th February, 2003 (w.e.f. 14-2-2003).
3. Clause (d) omitted by GS.R. 109 (E), dated 14th February, 2003 (w.e.f. 14-2-2003).
4. Ins. by G.S.R. 109 (E), daied 14th February, 2003 (w.e.f. 14-2-2003).
5. Subs, by G.S.R. 109 (E), dated 14th February, 2003 (w.e.f. 14-2-2003).
6. Subs, by G.S.R. 109 (E), da^ed 14th February, 2003 (w.e.f. 14-2-2003).
7. Subs, by G.S.R. 109 (E), dated 14th February, 2003 (w.e.f. 14-2-2003).
8. Subs, by G.S.R. 109 (E), dated 14th February, 2003 (w.e.f. 14-2-2003).
9. Ins. by C.S.R. 1(19 (E), dated 14th February, 2003 (w.e.f. 14-2-2013).
10. Subs, by G.S.R. 109 (E), dated 14th February, 2003 (w.e.f. 14-2-2003).
11. Subs, by G.S.R. 109 (E), dated 14th February, 2003 (w.e.f. 14-2-2003).
12. Subs, by G.S.R. 109 (E), dated 14th February, 2003 (w.e.f. 14-2-2013).
13. Subs, by G.S.R. 1(19 (E), dated 14th February, 2003 (w.e.f. 14-2-2003).
14. Subs, by G.S.R. 109 (E), dated 14th February, 2003 (w.e.f. 14-2-2003).

ANNEXURE – III

THE PRE-NATAL DIAGNOSTIC TECHNIQUES (REGULATION AND PREVENTION OF MISUSE) AMENDMENT ACT, 2002 (NO. 14 OF 2003)

17th January, 2003

An Act further to amend the Pre-natal Diagnostic Techniques (Regulation and Prevention of Misuse) Act, 1994.

Be it enacted by Parliament in the Fifty-third Year of the Republic of India as follows:

1. Short title and commencement –

(1) This Act may be called the Pre-natal Diagnostic Techniques (Regulation and Prevention of Misuse) Amendment Act, 2002.

(2) It shall come into force on such date as the Central Government may, by notification in the Official Gazette, appoint.

2. Substitution of long title–

In the Pre-natal Diagnostic Techniques (Regulation and Prevention of Misuse) Act, 1994 (57 of 1994) (hereinafter referred to as the principal Act), for the long title, the following long title shall be substituted, namely–

"An Act to provide for the prohibition of sex selection, before or after conception, and for regulation of pre-natal diagnostic techniques for the purposes of detecting genetic abnormalities or metabolic disorders or chromosomal abnormalities or certain congenital malformations or sex-linked disorders and for the prevention of their misuse for sex determination leading to female foeticide and for matters connected therewith or incidental thereto."

3. Amendment of section 1 –

In section 1 of the principal Act, in sub- section (1), for the words and brackets "the Pre-natal Diagnostic Techniques (Regulation and Prevention of Misuse)", the words and brackets "the Pre-conception and Pre-natal Diagnostic Techniques (Prohibition of sex Selection)" shall be substituted.

4. Amendment of section 2–

In section 2 of the principal Act, –

(i) after the clause (b), the following clauses shall be inserted, namely–

(ba) "conceptus" means any product of conception at any stage of development from fertilisation until birth including extra embryonic membranes as well as the embryo or foetus;

(bb) "embryo" means a developing human organism after fertilisation till the end of eight weeks (fifty-six days);

(bc) "foetus" means a human organism during the period of its development beginning on the fifty-seventh day following fertilisation or creation (excluding any time in which its development has been suspended) and ending at the birth;

(ii) in clause (d), the following Explanation shall be added, namely–

Explanation– For the purposes of this clause, "Genetic Clinic" includes a vehicle, where ultrasound machine or imaging machine or scanner or other equipment capable of determining sex of the foetus or a portable equipment which has the potential for detection of sex during pregnancy or selection of sex before conception, is used;

(iii) in clause (e), the following Explanation shall be added, namely:

Explanation– For the purposes of this clause, "Genetic Laboratory" includes a place where ultrasound machine or imaging machine or scanner or other equipment capable of determining sex of the foetus or a portable equipment which has the potential for detection of sex during pregnancy or selection of sex before conception, is used.;

(iv) for clause (g), the following clause shall be substituted, namely–

(g) "medical geneticist" includes a person who possesses a degree or diploma in genetic science in the fields of sex selection and pre-natal diagnostic techniques or has experience of not less than two years in any of these fields after obtaining–

(i) any one of the medical qualifications recognised under the Indian Medical Council Act, 1956 (102 of 1956); or

(ii) a post-graduate degree in biological sciences;

(v) for clause (i), the following clause shall be substituted, namely–

(i) "pre-natal diagnostic procedures" means all gynaecological or obstetrical or medical procedures such as ultrasonography, foetoscopy, taking or removing samples of amniotic fluid, chorionic villi, embryo, blood or any other tissue or fluid of a man, or of a woman before or after conception, for being sent to a Genetic Laboratory or Genetic Clinic for conducting any type of analysis or pre-natal diagnostic tests for selection of sex before or after conception;;

(vi) for clause (k), the following clause shall be substituted, namely–

(k) "pre-natal diagnostic test" means ultrasonography or any test or analysis of amniotic fluid, chorionic villi, blood or any tissue or fluid of a pregnant woman or conceptus conducted to detect genetic or metabolic disorders or chromosomal abnormalities or congenital anomalies or haemoglobinopathies or sex-linked diseases;

(vii) after clause (n), the following clauses shall be inserted, namely–

(o) "sex selection" includes any procedure, technique, test or administration or prescription or provision of anything for the purpose of ensuring or increasing the probability that an embryo will be of a particular sex;

(p) "sonologist or imaging specialist" means a person who possesses any one of the medical qualifications recognised under the Indian Medical Council Act, 1956 or who possesses a post-graduate qualification in ultrasonography or imaging techniques or radiology;

(q) "State Board" means a State Supervisory Board or a Union territory Supervisory Board constituted under section 16A;

(r) "State Government" in relation to Union territory with Legislature means the Administrator of that Union territory appointed by the President under article 239 of Constitution.[1]

5. Amendment of section 3–

In section 3 of the principal Act, for clause (2), the following clause shall be substituted, namely–

(2) "no Genetic Counseling Centre or Genetic Laboratory or Genetic Clinic shall employ or cause to be employed or take services of any person, whether on honorary basis or on payment who does not possess the qualifications as may be prescribed."

6. Insertion of new sections 3A and 3B–

After section 3 of the principal Act, the following sections shall be inserted, namely–

3A. Prohibition of sex selection— No person, including a specialist or a term of specialists in the field of infertility, shall conduct or cause to be conducted or aid in conducting by himself or by any other person, sex selection on a woman or a man or on both or on any tissue, embryo, conceptus, fluid or gametes derived from either or both of them.

3B. Prohibition on sale of ultrasound machine, etc., to persons, laboratories, clinics, etc., not registered under the Act. — No person shall sell any ultrasound machine or imaging machine or scanner or any other equipment capable of detecting sex of the foetus to any Genetic Counseling Centre, Genetic Laboratory, Genetic Clinic or any other person not registered under the Act."

7. Amendment of section 4–

In section 4 of the principal Act, for Clause (3) & (4), the following clauses shall be substituted, namely–

(3) no pre-natal diagnostic techniques shall be used or conducted unless the person qualified to do so is satisfied for reasons to be recorded in writing that any of the following conditions are fulfilled, namely:

(i) age of the pregnant woman is above thirty-five years;

(ii) the pregnant woman has undergone two or more spontaneous abortions or foetal loss;

(iii) the pregnant woman had been exposed to potentially toratogenic agents such as drugs, radiation, infection or chemicals;

(iv) the pregnant woman or her spouse has a family history of mental retardation or physical deformities such as, spasticity or any other genetic disease;

(v) any other condition as may be specified by the Board:

Provided mat the person conducting ultrasonography on a pregnant woman shall keep complete record thereof in the clinic in such manner, as may be prescribed, and any deficiency or inaccuracy found therein shall amount to contravention of the provisions of section 5 or section 6 unless contrary is proved by the person conducting such ultrasonography;

(4) no person including a relative or husband of the pregnant woman shall seek or encourage the conduct of any pre-natal diagnostic techniques on her except for the purposes specified in clause (2);

(5) no person including a relative or husband of a woman shall seek or encourage the conduct of any sex-selection technique on her or him or both."

8. Amendment of section 5 –

In section 5 of the principal Act, for sub-section, (2) the following sub-section shall be substituted, namely:

(2) "No person including the person conducting pre-natal diagnostic procedures shall communicate to the pregnant woman concerned or her relatives or any other person the sex of the foetus by words, signs, or in any other manner."

9. Amendment of section 6 –

In section 6 of the principal Act, after clause (b), the following clause shall be inserted, namely:

(c) no person shall, by whatever means, cause or allow to be selection of sex before or after conception."

10. Amendment of section 7–

In section 7 of the principal Act, –

(i) in sub-section (2), for clause (c), the following clause shall be substituted, namely:

(c) three members to be appointed by the Central Government to represent the Ministries of Central Government in charge of Women and Child Development, Department of Legal Affairs or Legislative Department in the Ministry of Law and Justice, and Indian System of Medicine and Homoeopathy, ex officio,

(ii) in clause (e), for sub-clause (ii), the following sub-clause shall be substituted, namely′–

(ii) eminent gynaecologist and obstetrician or expert of *stri-roga or prasuti-tantra.*"

11. Amendment of section 14–

In section 14 of the principal Act, for clause (f), the following clause shall be substituted, namely–

"(f) has, in the opinion of the Central Government, been associated with the use or promotion of pre-natal diagnositic technique for determination of sex or with any sex selection technique.".

12. Amendment of section 15–

In section "15 of the principal Act, the so shall be inserted, namely:

"Provided that no member other than an *ex officio* member shall be appointed for more than two consecutive terms."

13.Substitution of new section for section 16–

For section 16 of the principal Act, the following section shall be substituted, namely–

16. Functions of the Board–The Board shall have the following functions, namely:

(i) to advise the Central Government on policy matters relating to use of pre-natal diagnostic techniques, sex selection techniques and against their misuse;

(ii) to review and monitor implementation of the Act and rules made there under and recommend to the Central Government changes in the said Act and rules;

(iii) to create public awareness against the practice of pre-conception sex selection and pre-natal determination of sex of foetus leading to female foeticide;

(iv) to lay down code of conduct to be observed by persons at Genetic Counseling Centres, Genetic Laboratories and Genetic Clinics;

(v) to oversee the performance of various bodies constituted under the Act and take appropriate steps to ensure its proper and effective implementation;

(vi) any other functions as may be prescribed under the Act.".

14. Insertion of new section 16A–

After section 16 of the principal Act, the following section shall be inserted, namely:

16A. Constitution of State Supervisory Board and Union territory Supervisory Board –

(1) Each State and Union territory having Legislature shall constitute a Board to be known as the State Supervisory Board or the Union territory Supervisory Board, as the case may be, which shall have the following functions:

(i) to create public awareness against the practice of pre-conception sex selection and pre-natal determination of the sex of the foetus leading to female foeticide in the State;

(ii) to review the activities of the Appropriate Authorities in the State and recommend appropriate action against them;

(iii) to monitor the implementation of provisions of the Act and the rules and make suitable recommendations relating thereto, to the Board;

(iv) to send such consolidated reports as may be prescribed in respect of the various activities undertaken in the State under the Act to the Board and the Central Government; and

(v) any other functions as may be prescribed under the Act.

(2) The State Board shall consist of, –

(a) the Minister in charge of Health and Family Welfare in the State, who shall be the Chairperson, ex officio;

(b) Secretary in charge of the Department of Health and Family Welfare who shall be the Vice-Chairperson, ex officio;

(c) Secretaries or Commissioners in charge of Departments of Women and Child Development, Social Welfare, Law and Indian System of Medicines and Homoeopathy, ex officid, or their representatives;

(d) Director of Health and Family Welfare or Indian System of Medicines and Homoeopathy of the State Government, *ex officio;*

(e) three women members of Legislative Assembly or Legislative Council;

(f) ten members to be appointed by the State Government out of which two each shall be from the following categories, –

(i) eminent social scientists and legal experts;

(ii) eminent women activists from non-governmental organisations or otherwise;

(iii) eminent gynaecologists arid obstetricians or experts of *stri- roga or prasuti-tantm;*

(iv) eminent paediatricians or medical geneticists;

(v) eminent radiologists or sonologists;

(g) an officer not below the rank of Joint Director in charge of Family Welfare, who shall be the Member Secretary, ex officio.

(3) The State Board shall meet at least once in four months.

(4) The term of office of a member, other than an ex officio member, shall be three years.

(5) If a vacancy occurs in the office of any member other then an *ex officio* member, it shall be filled by making fresh appointment.

(6) If a member of the Legislative Assembly or member of the Legislative Council who is a member of the State Board, becomes Minister or Speaker or Deputy Speaker of the Legislative Assembly or Chairperson or Deputy Chairperson of the Legislative Council, she shall cease to be a member of the State Board.

(7) One-third of the total number of members of the State Board shall constitute the quorum.

(8) The State Board may co-opt a member as and when required, provided that the number of co-opted members does not exceed on third of the total strength of the State Board.

(9) The co-opted members shall have the same powers and functions as other members except the right to vote and shall abide by the rules and regulations.

(10) In respect of matters not specified in this section, the State Board shall follow procedures and conditions as are applicable to the Board.

15. Amendment of section 17–

In section 17 of the principal Act, –

(i) in sub-section (3), for clause (a), the following clause shall be substituted, namely:

(a) when appointed for the whole of the State or the Union territory, consisting of the following three members–

(i) an officer of or above the rank of the Joint Director of Health and Family Welfare–Chairperson;

(ii) an eminent woman representing women's organisation; and

(iii) an officer of Law Department of the State or the Union territory concerned:

Provided that it shall be the duty of the State or the Union territory concerned to constitute multi-member State or Union territory level Appropriate Authority within three months of the coming into force of the Pre-natal Diagnostic Techniques (Regulation and Prevention of Misuse) Amendment Act, 2002:

Provided further that any vacancy occurring therein shall be filled within three months of the occurrence."

(ii) in sub-section (4), after clause (d), the following clauses shall be inserted, namely:

(e) to take a appropriate legal action against the use of any sex selection brought technique by any person at any place, *suo moto* or brought to its notice and also to initiate independent investigations in such matter;

(f) to create public awareness against tine practice of sex selection or prenatal determination of sex;

(g) to supervise the implementation of the provisions of the Act and rules,

(h) to recommend to the Board and State Boards modifications required in the rules in accordance with changes in technology or social conditions;

(i) to take action on the recommendations of the Advisory Committee made after investigation of complaint for suspension or cancellation of registration.";

(iii) for sub-section (7), the following sub-section shall be substituted, namely:

(7) No person who has been associated with the use or promotion of pre-natal diagnostic techniques for determination of sex or sex selection shall be appointed as a member of the Advisory Committee.

16. Insertion of new section 17A–

After section 17 of the principal Act, the following section shall be inserted, namely:

17 A. Powers of Appropriate Authorities.—The Appropriate Authority shall have the powers in respect of the following matters, namely:

(a) summoning of any person who is in possession of any information relating to violation of the provisions of this Act or the rules made there under;

(b) production of any document or material object relating to clause (a);

(c) issuing search warrant for any place suspected to be indulging in sex selection techniques or pre-natal sex determination; and

(d) any other matter which may be prescribed.

17. Amendment of section 18–

In section 18 of the principal Act, for sub-section (1), the following sub-section shall be substituted, namely:

(1) No person shall open any Genetic Counseling Centre, Genetic Laboratory or Genetic Clinic, including clinic, laboratory or centre having ultrasound or imaging machine or scanner or any other technology capable of undertaking determination of sex of foetus and sex selection, or render services to any of them,

after the commencement of the Pre-natal Diagnostic Techniques (Regulation and Prevention of Misuse) Amendment Act, 2002 unless such Centre, Laboratory or Clinic is duly registered under the Act.

18. Substitution of new section for section 22–

For section 22 of the principal Act, the following section shall be substituted, namely:

22. Prohibition of advertisement relating to pre-conception and pre nnt.nl determination of sex and punishment for contravention–

(1) No person, organisation, Genetic Counseling Centre, Genetic Laboratory or centre having ultrasound machine or imaging machine or scanner or any other technology capable of undertaking determination of sex of the foetus or sex selection shall issue, publish, distribute, communicate or cause to be issued, published, distributed or communicated any advertisement, in any form, including internet, regarding facilities of prenatal determination of sex or sex selection before conception available at such Centre, Laboratory, Clinic or at any other place.

(2) No person or organisation including Genetic Counseling Centre, Genetic Laboratory or Genetic Clinic shall issue, publish, distribute, communicate or cause to be issued, published, distributed or communicated any advertisement in any manner regarding pre-natal determination or preconception selection of sex by any means whatsoever, scientific or otherwise.

(3) Any person who contravenes the provisions of sub-section (1) or sub-section (2) shall be punishable with imprisonment for a term which may extend to three years and with fine which may extend to ten thousand rupees.

Explanation–For the purposes of this section, "advertisement" includes any notice, circular, label, wrapper or any other document including advertisement through internet or any other media in electronic or print form and also includes any visible representation made by means of any hoarding, wall-painting, signal, light, sound, smoke or gas.

19. Amendment of section 23–

In section 23 of the principal Act, for sub-sections (2) and (3), the following sub-sections shall be substituted, namely:

(2) The name of the registered medical practitioner shall be reported by the Appropriate Authority to the State Medical Council concerned for taking necessary action including suspension of tine registration if the charges are framed by the court and till the case is disposed of and on conviction for removal of his name from the register of the Council for a period of five years for the first offence and permanently for the subsequent offence.

(3) Any person who seeks the aid of any Genetic Counseling Centre, Genetic Laboratory, Genetic Clinic or ultrasound clinic or imaging clinic or of a medical geneticist, gynecologist, sonologist or imaging specialist or registered medical practitioner or any other person for sex selection or for conducting pre-natal diagnostic techniques on any pregnant women for the purposes other than those specified in sub-section (2) of section 4, he shall, be punishable with imprisonment for a term which may extend to three years and with fine which may extend to fifty thousand rupees for the first offence and for any subsequent offence with imprisonment which may extend to five years and with fine which may extend to one lakh rupees.

(4) For the removal of doubts, it is hereby provided that the provisions of sub-section (3) shall not apply to the woman who was compelled to undergo such diagnostic techniques or such selection."

20. Substitution of new section for section 24–

For section 24 of the principal Act, the following section shall be substituted, namely–

24. Presumption in the case of conduct of pre-natal diagnostic techniques. – Notwithstanding anything contained in the Indian Evidence Act, 1872, the court shall presume unless the contrary is proved that the pregnant woman was compelled by her husband or any other relative, as the case may be, to undergo pre-natal diagnostic technique for the purposes other than those specified in sub-section (2) of section 4 and such person shall be liable for

abetment of offence under sub-section (3) of section 23 and shall be punishable for the offence specified under that section."

21. Amendment of section 28–

In section 28 of the principal Act, in sub-section (1), in clause (b), for the words "thirty days", the words "fifteen days" shall be substituted.

22. Amendment of section 30–

In section 30 of the principal Act, for sub-section (1), the following sub-section shall be substituted, namely–

(1) If the Appropriate Authority has reason to believe that an offence under this Act has been or is being committed at any Genetic Counseling Centre, Genetic Laboratory, Genetic Clinic or any other place, such Authority or any officer authorised in this behalf may, subject to such rules as may be prescribed, enter and search at all reasonable times with such assistance, if any, as such Authority or officer considers necessary, such Genetic Counseling Centre, Genetic Laboratory, Genetic Clinic or any other place and examine any record, register, document, book, pamphlet, advertisement or any other material object found therein and seize and seal the same if such Authority or officer has reason to believe that it may furnish evidence of the commission of an offence punishable under this Act".

23. Insertion of new section 31 A–

After section 31 of the principal Act, the following section shall be inserted, namely–

31 A. Removal of difficulties. - (I) If any difficulty arises in giving effect to the provisions of the Pre-natal Diagnostic Techniques (Regulation and Prevention of Misuse) Amendment Act, 2002, the Central Government may, by order published in the Official Gazette, make such provisions not inconsistent with the provisions of the said Act as appear to it to be necessary or expedient for removing the difficulty:

Provided that no order shall be made under this section after the expiry of a period of three years from the date of commencement of the Pre-natal Diagnostic Techniques (Regulation and Prevention of Misuse) Amendment Act, 2002.

(2) Every order made under this section shall be laid, as soon as may be after it is made, before each House of Parliament."

24. Amendment of section 32–

In section 32 of the principal Act, in subsection (2),–

(i) for clause (i), the following clauses shall be substituted, namely:

(i) the minimum qualifications for persons employed at a registered Genetic Counseling Centre, Genetic Laboratory or Genetic Clinic under clause (2) of section 3;

(ia) the manner in which the person conducting ultrasonography on a pregnant woman shall keep record thereof in the clinic under the proviso to sub-section (3) of section 4;

(ii) after clause (iv), the following clauses shall be inserted, namely:

(iva) code of conduct to be observed by persons working at Genetic Counseling Centres, Genetic Laboratories and Genetic Clinics to be laid down by the Central Supervisory Board under clause (iv) of section 16;

(ivb) the manner in which reports shall be furnished by the State and Union Territory Supervisory Boards to the Board and the Central Government in respect of various activities undertaken in the State under the Act under clause (iv) of sub-section (1) of section 16A;

(ivc) empowering the Appropriate Authority in any other matter under clause (d) of section 17A.

ANNEXURE – IV

PRE-CONCEPTION AND PRE-NATAL DIAGNOSTIC TECHNIQUES (PROHIBITION OF SEX SELECTION AMENDMENT RULES, 2014) MINISTRY OF HEALTH AND FAMILY WELFARE (DEPARTMENT OF HEALTH AND FAMILY WELFARE) NOTIFICATION, NEW DELHI, THE 24TH FEBRUARY, 2014

G.S.R. 119(E).-In exercise of the powers conferred by section 32 of the Pre-conception and Pre-natal Diagnostic Techniques (Prohibition of Sex Selection) Act, 1994 (57 of 1994), the Central Government hereby makes the following rules further to amend the Pre-conception and Pre-natal Diagnostic Techniques (prohibition of Sex Selection) Rules, 1996, namely:

(1) These rules may be called the Pre-conception and Pre-natal Diagnostic Techniques (Prohibition of Sex Selection) Amendment Rules, 2014.

(2) They shall come into force on the date of their publication in the Official Gazette.

  (i) In the Pre-conception and Pre-natal Diagnostic Techniques (Prohibition of Sex Selection) Rules, 1996, after rule 18, the following rule shall be inserted, namely:-

18-A Code of Conduct to be observed by Appropriate

Authorities- (1) All the Appropriate Authorities including the State, District and Sub-district notified under the Act, inter-alia, shall observe the following general code of conduct, namely:

(i) maintain dignity, and integrity at all times;

(ii) observe and implement the provisions of the Act and Rules in a balanced and standardised manner in the course of their work;

(iii) conduct their work in a just manner without any bias or a perceived presumption of guilt;

(iv) refrain from making any comments which demean individuals on the basis of gender, race, religion;

(v) delegate his or her powers by administrative order to any authorised officer in his or her absence and preserve the order of authorisation as documentary proof for further action.

(2) All the Appropriate Authorities including the State, District and Sub-district notified under the Act, inter-alia, shall observe the following Conduct for Advisory Committees, namely:

(i) ensure that the re-constitution, functions and other relevant matters related to advisory committee shall be in accordance with the provisions of the Advisory Committee Rules, 1996;

(ii) ensure that a person who is the part of investigating machinery in cases under the Pre-conception and Pre-natal Diagnostic Techniques (Prohibition of Sex Selection) Act, 1994 (57 of 1994), shall not be nominated or appointed as a member of the Advisory Committee;

(iii) ensure that the process of filling up of vacancies in Advisory Committee shall start at least ninety days before the probable date of the occurrence of vacancy;

(iv) ensure that no person shall participate as a member or a legal expert of the Advisory Committee if he or she has conflict of interest;

(v) conduct frequent meetings of the Advisory Committee to expedite the decisions regarding renewal, cancellation and suspension of registration.

(3) All the Appropriate Authorities including the State, District and Sub-district notified under the Act, inter-alia, shall observe the following conduct for processing of complaint and investigation, namely:

(i) maintain appropriate diaries in support of registration of each of the complaint or case under the Act;

(ii) attend to all complaints and maintain transparency in the follow-up action of the complaints;

(iii) investigate all the complaints within twenty four hours of receipt of the complaint and complete the investigation within forty-eight hours of receipt of such compliant;

(iv) as far as possible, not involve police for investigating cases under the Act as the cases are tried as complaint cases under the Code of Criminal Procedure, 1973 (2 of 1974).

(4) All the Appropriate Authorities including the State, District and Sub-district notified under the Act, inter-alia, shall observe the following conduct for registration and renewal of applications under the Act, namely:

(i) dispose of the application for renewal and new registration within a period of seventy days from the date of receipt of application;

(ii) ensure that no application for fresh registration or renewal is accepted if any case is pending in any court against the applicant.

(5) All the Appropriate Authorities including the State, District and Sub-district notified under the Act, inter-alia, shall observe the following conduct for Legal Action, namely:

(i) ensure that protection and expenses of witness shall be met from the registration amount collected;

(ii) ensure that all the notifications of the Government be produced in original in the court and a copy of the same be preserved;

(iii) ensure that while filing the cases, all the papers, records, statements, evidence, panchnama and other material objects attached to the case file shall be in original;

(iv) suspend the certificate of registration in the course of taking legal action of seizure and sealing of the facility;

(v) ensure that there shall be no violation of the provisions of the Medical Termination Pregnancy Act, 1971 (34 of 1971) and the Rules made there-under while implementing the provisions of the Pre-conception and Prenatal Diagnostic Techniques (Prohibition of Sex Selection) Rules, 1996;

(vi) take immediate action for filing appeal, revision or other proceeding in higher courts in case of order of acquittal within a period of thirty days but not later than fifteen days of receipt of the order of acquittal.

(6) All the Appropriate Authorities including the State, District and Sub-district notified under the Act, inter-alia, shall submit quarterly progress report to the Government of India through State Government and maintain Form H for keeping the information of all the registrations made readily available.

(7) All the Appropriate Authorities including the State, District and Sub-district notified under the Act, inter-alia, shall observe the following regulation of ultrasound equipments, namely:

- (i) monitor the sales and import of ultrasound machines including portable or buyback, assembled, gift, scrap or demo;
- (ii) ensure regular quarterly reports from ultrasound manufacturers, dealers, wholesalers and retailers and any person dealing with the sales of ultrasound machines at the State level;
- (iii) conduct periodical survey and audit of all the ultrasound machines sold and operating in the State or district to identify the unregistered machines;
- (iv) file complaint against any owner of the unregistered ultrasound machine and against the seller of the unregistered ultrasound machine.

(8) AU the Appropriate Authorities including the State, District and Sub-district notified under the Act, inter-alia, shall observe the following conduct for inspection and monitoring, namely:

- (i) conduct regular inspection of all the registered facilities once in every ninety days and shall preserve the inspection report as documentary evidence and a copy of the same be handed over to the owner of facility inspected and obtain acknowledgement in respect of the inspection;
- (ii) place all the inspection reports once in three months before the Advisory Committee for follow up action;
- (iii) maintain bimonthly progress report containing number of cases filed and persons convicted, registration made, suspended or cancelled, medical licenses cancelled, suspended, inspections conducted, Advisory Committee meetings held at the district level and quarterly progress report at the State level;
- (iv) (a) procure the copy of the charges framed within seven days and in the case of doctors, the details of the charges framed shall be submitted within seven days of the receipt of copy of charges framed to the State Medical Council;

  (b) procure the certified copy of the order of conviction as soon as possible and in the case of conviction of the doctors, the certified copy of the order of conviction shall be submitted within seven days of the receipt of copy of the order of conviction.

(9) AU the Appropriate Authorities including the State, District and Sub-district notified under the Act, inter-alia, shall observe the following conduct for accountability, namely:

(i) obtain prior sanction or approval of the Government of India for any resolution concerning the implementation of the provisions of the Act;

(ii) take action, if any, required under the Act and immediately on receipt of notice under clause (b) of subsection (1) of section 28 of the Act and if he or she fails to do so, shall not be entitled for the protection under section 31 of the said Act and defend the case in his or her own capacity and at his or her own cost.

(10) All the Appropriate Authorities including the State, District and Sub-district notified under the Act, inter-alia, shall follow the following financial guidance, namely:

(i) maintain a separate and independent bank account operated by two officers jointly, at all levels ;

(ii) ensure transparency and adherence to standard Government financial norms for disbursement of money.

[F. No. v. 11011/8/2013-PNDT]

Dr. Rakesh Kumar, Jt. Secy.

Note: The principal rules were published in the Gazette of India, Part II, Section 3, Sub-section (i), vide G.S.R 1(E), dated the 1st January, 1996 and amended, by notification No. G.S.R. 109(E), dated the 14th February, 2003; G.S.R. 426(E), dated the 31st May, 2011; G.S.R. 80(E), dated the 7th February, 2012; G.S.R. 418(E), dated the 4th June, 2012; G.S.R. 13(E), dated the 9th January, 2014 and G.S.R. 77(E) dated 31st January, 2014.

Bibliography

Adam Jones & Gendercide Watch 1999-2000.

Census of India

Croll E (2000) Endangered Daughters, London, Routledge

Daughters of Gardeners (2007) Directed by Karina Marceau Montreal: Cinefete.

Gautam Chikermane, "To Save the Girl Child Invest" Indian Express, March 30, 2006

Indu Grewal and J. Kishore, International Humanist and Ethical Union

Kollor T M (1990) Female infanticide: A Psychological analysis. Grass Roots Action, Special issue on Girl Child April 3, and pp 3.

Matrubhoomi: A Nationa without women (2005) directed by Manish Jha, Patrick Sobelman, Punkej Kharbanda Production.

Patel, T. (2007) Sex-Selective Abortion in India. New Delhi, India: Sage Publications India Pvt.

Rai U (1992) Female infanticide rampant in Salem. Indian Express, July 4. pp. 4

Srivastava R D (2000) Girls are second-class citizens everywhere. The Times of India, January 17: 3.

Sex-selective Abortion in India edited by Tulsi Patel

The Pre-birth Elimination of Females in India, Ending the Practice: Changing the Mindset, A National Advocacy Strategy Draft, June 17, 2002

Journals

Dube L (1983) Misadventures in amniocentesis. Economic and Political Weekly 40 (2): 279-80.

Kumari R (1995) Rural female adolescence: Indian scenario. Social Change 25 (2): 177-88.Mane P N (1991) Socialization of Hindu women in their childhood: An analysis of Literature. The Journal of Family Welfare 52 (1): 81-96.

Manjeet Rathe, "Eradicate Scourge of Female Foeticide", People's Democracy, Vol XXV, No 39, September 30

Manmeet Kaur, "Female Foeticide:A Sociological Perspective", The Journal of Family Welfare, Vol 39(1), March 1993

Manohar Agnani (Dr) is an IAS officer of MP cadre. He can be reached at manooagnani@yahoo.com) 2007 Indo-Asian News Service Express, April 5, 2006

Puri N (1998) The girl child in India. The Journal of Family Welfare 44 (3): 1-8.

Sangeeta Cheetu, "Growing Menace of Female Foeticide in India", Indian Socio-Legal Journal, Vol. XVII (1 and 2), 1991

Yadav S and Badari V S (1999) Gender Preference and Anxiety of Pregnant Women. The Indian Journal of Social Work 60 (4): 538-51.

Websites

External links open in a new window and take you to a non-UNICEF web site.

foeticide.blogspot.com

http://census2011.nic.in

http://censusmp.nic.in

http://www.christiancadre.org/member_contrib/cp_infanticide.html.

http://www.iosworld.org/abortion-vs-female-foeticide.html

ideajournal.com by A jinder walia

legalserviceindia.com

m.timesofindia.com

maharasthraweb.com/haryana/foeticide

Index